Wabi Sabi Simple

Create beauty.

Value imperfection.

Live deeply.

Richard R. Powell

Adams Media
Avon, Massachusetts

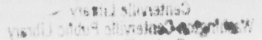
Published by

Adams Media, an F+W Publications Company

57 Littlefield Street, Avon, MA 02322 U.S.A.

www.adamsmedia.com

ISBN: 1-59337-178-0

Printed in Canada.

J I H G F E D C B A

Library of Congress Cataloging-in-Publication Data
Powell, Richard R.
Wabi sabi simple / Richard R. Powell.
p.   cm.
ISBN 1-59337-178-0
1. Conduct of life. 2. Wabi. 3. Sabi. I. Title.

BJ1581.2.P69 2004
170--dc22

2004005960

This publication is designed to provide accurate and authoritative information with regard to the subject matter covered. It is sold with the understanding that the publisher is not engaged in rendering legal, accounting, or other professional advice. If legal advice or other expert assistance is required, the services of a competent professional person should be sought.
—From a *Declaration of Principles* jointly adopted by a Committee of the American Bar Association and a Committee of Publishers and Associations

Many of the designations used by manufacturers and sellers to distinguish their products are claimed as trademarks. Where those designations appear in this book and Adams Media was aware of a trademark claim, the designations have been printed with initial capital letters.

Interior photograph © Photodisc. Kanji characters illustrated by Graphic Expressions.

This book is available at quantity discounts for bulk purchases.
For information, call 1-800-872-5627.

Dedication

for my father who taught me to fish from the back of the canoe and my mother who gave me the right books at the right time

Acknowledgments

Thanks to: my wife Marilyn, who read each draft and offered welcome clarity; my children Matthew and Graham, who were reasonably quiet and unreasonably patient; Michael Jewell, who taught me to notice at the third level; Ron Fuller, who regularly shared both sea and tea with me; John Woods, of CWL Publishing Enterprises, who found and encouraged me; Kate Epstein, who envisioned this project and exemplified wabi sabi in her editing; and the Vancouver Island Regional Library, which supplied the books I needed month after month.

While doing research for this book I observed, not for the first time, that libraries are more than repositories and archives. They are a kind of parkland where wabi sabi grows wild.

Contents

Introduction

THE COMPLEXITY OF LIFE can mask its poignancy. The web of daily tasks and events can seem so manifold, so knotty and tangled, that the deeper richness contained within them gets overshadowed, lost in the labyrinth of scheduling, obscured by the preoccupation with efficiency. The ongoing attempt to stay on track, to balance multiple demands for time, eventually conditions us to accept dizziness as normal, and multiple distractions as a daily inevitability.

We get good at screening calls, scanning e-mails, and multitasking. We grow used to overstimulation, resigned to clutter and excess. Instead of periods of busyness, we find that the details of each opportunity pile up like snow during a very long winter. Each flake seems so small and harmless, lovely on its own as it drifts from the sky, but when there are several feet of those flakes all piled up, those little details become a blanket of obfuscation.

Are you feeling snowed over, snowed in, buried? Have you just shoveled out the driveway, only to look up and see the snowplow coming with its blade pointed right at you? Are you longing for a Christmas break in the "detail deluge," a holiday respite from the snow load of particulars and possessions? Maybe you have begun to realize that the warmth and security that goes along with procuring the necessities of life can also be accompanied by the colder precipitation of multiple possessions. Perhaps in the bracing reality of making a living you have lost touch with the warm pulse of life. Don't worry, that pulse is still there, still rhyming each moment with a rhythm of meaning. All those details, meetings, appointments, tasks, and obligations can be recognized as the colorful paper, wrappings, and trappings that surround subtler gifts. Understood in this way, each busy life can provide a steady supply of hidden presents. What this book helps you see is that to get to these presents you simply need to be present inside the wrapping.

Many wise traditions know the importance of finding a balance between action and stillness. One way of achieving that balance is by a simple yet profound way of living called wabi sabi.

It is a way that is natural, drawing close to the real world, and relaxing perpetually into the beautiful patterns that exist there. It is an ancient way, tried and practiced over many years. It is an intuitive way that wells up within anyone who looks for it. It only needs to be recognized and named. Wabi sabi is a way of life that appreciates and accepts complexity while at the same time values simplicity. It nurtures all that is authentic by acknowledging three simple realities: nothing lasts, nothing is finished, and nothing is perfect. To accept these realities is to accept contentment as the maturation of happiness, and to acknowledge that clarity and grace can be found in genuine unvarnished existence. Filled with subtlety and depth, this way is a river flowing toward and away from you, and always within you.

侘寂

Wabi Sabi

One
What wabi sabi is

turn off the engine

radio stops abruptly

cricket song instead

BEFORE FREUD NAMED THE EGO, people were egotistical. Before Newton called it gravity, people dropped things, but they didn't say, "Hey look, gravity." Before Darwin named it evolution, no one talked about selective adaptation, but they bred horses and cattle and pigeons and peas and corn and wheat and a host of other things, evolving them toward an outcome they wanted.

Wabi sabi is like ego, gravity, and evolution; you may know it well, but have never named it.

The words are Japanese, but the reality behind the words runs like a handspun thread through the tapestry of most people's lives. Though it is widely felt and fostered, it is rarely talked about, except indirectly. In English we talk about a fishing village having "rustic charm," or we might comment on the "lodge appeal" of a summer cabin. One of the nicest qualities of wabi sabi is that it is felt in the bones, and often is associated with fond memories of childhood experiences. My first experience with wabi sabi occurred when I was four years old.

Dust: waking to the wonder of decay

I was little and there was no thought of a clock or calendar or any reason for one. My days started with opening my eyes and ended with closing them. I was free to wake and listen to the sounds of morning—my mother at work in the kitchen, those familiar and reassuring sounds that told me she was there, safely tucked into normal, predictable rhythms beyond comment. I padded out of my bedroom into the hardwood hallway that led to the kitchen. And there, for the first time in my stretchy little life, I saw, shimmering in a shaft of honey-colored air, golden motes of dust floating, spinning, and throwing me light. I reached out my hand into the silent, sparkling light and watched it swirl around my movement, specks too small to grasp. When I think about it now, it is as if plasma-bright tendrils, the color of cut apples, were touching my outstretched hands, revealing what I could never hold. My gaze traced the direction back to the window in the kitchen door, so high in the door that all I ever saw through it was sky, and treetops moving in a breeze. Now this flat, hard, shiny square was letting in magic, too bright to look at directly, but a wonder in the air. A burbling exclamation, a question, and then my mother explained, "Oh yes, isn't the light beautiful?"

"But what is it?" I asked.

"Dust, playing in the light, bits of things, bits of the floor, bits of the walls, bits of soil from outside, bits of your father's coat, bits of skin, bits of dog hair, bits of pollen from the plants, lots of little bits of everything."

This was too much to imagine, too much to think that the world was coming apart into such beauty. Then, a sort of creeping realization as I stood breathing into the golden chaos, my breath moving the motes, becoming visible for the first time, and then the rush of motes toward me as I breathed in, drawing them into myself: the floor, the walls, the soil, father's coat, skin, dog, pollen, everything. Where did it go when it was inside me? Breathing out, I, too, was adding myself, maybe, to the golden phantom. To wake into morning, into meaning, this childhood wonder was my dusted beginning in wabi sabi.

Now, in my bright, tight life I search, yearn, claw after that velvet box of time when nothing intruded on wonder, bare as an empty boat, not even the thought of it. This boy in memory is still inside, stretched and grown, but I look out of the same eyes, to these small things, and wonder, asking over again, "What is it? What are all these bits of me waiting to be gone?" This core of seeing yourself connected to the world, and seeing it coming apart and growing together, this exchange of death for more life is the blood that pumps through wabi sabi. It is the color of flowers dancing on the floor that allows you to hold open thoughts and take the raw and tender attention of wonder, and move it to the subtle and fragile act of naming. When you can hold this in appreciation without comment or judgment, when you can allow the thing named to go on being nameless, this is wabi sabi.

Wabi sabi is a secret you already know

I never met my grandfather. I heard stories about him, an adventurer who came to the West for the Gold Rush, an able journeyman who built houses, cabinets, and furniture. He passed on to my father, who passed on to me, the secret. They didn't know the secret by name; instead, they lived the secret. The secret is wabi sabi. I know my grandfather knew the secret because I have something of his that shows it, a wooden chair that he made. It is a somewhat plain chair, proper and upright, unadorned and functional. Yet it has subtlety. The back is nicely curved and easy to lean against. The back legs curve backward near the floor, providing the right angle to support the large area above. And it has patina, that rich deep look that wood gets over time. It is a sort of chestnut brown with mottled ribbons and swirls. It reminds me of Shaker furniture, that renowned craftsmanship of simple lines and simple elegance. The arms are flat and unremarkable, but the left arm is worn. Someone, or perhaps everyone who sat in it, pivoted on that arm as they got up, wearing away the finish and eventually the wood itself. It gives me pleasure every time I look at it.

Old wooden chairs are in almost everyone's life. There is nothing particularly special about them, except that they are seldom really seen. Most people overlook them, preferring the excitement surrounding new things. The new car, the new carpet, the new clothes, the new appliance; these things capture our attention because the human animal thrives on novelty and the human brain is a mapmaker. When a picture, for example, is first brought home, we look at it and admire it. Then, over time, the brain relegates it to mapish location, blending it into the background of life. And there is nothing wrong with this, except that over time things pile up. Many new things now are made to be disposable because consumerism is out of control, and there simply isn't enough room in our homes in which to stuff everything. But disposability is not the answer; a change of heart is the answer.

Filling life with wabi sabi might be as simple as emptying it of clutter. Wabi sabi cannot be contained in anything square, boxy, or bright, nor can it ever be modular. Quality control kills it, and uniformity negates it. It has to be authentic, genuine, and natural. It perishes under refinement, and sameness wilts it. Acquiring large quantities of wabi sabi objects defeats the purpose, because central to their appeal is their uniqueness, their one-of-a-kind feel, and the way they make life less institutional, less grandiose, less highfalutin'. Having lots of wabi sabi is a contradiction.

Origin of the phrase

Wabi sabi is Japanese. Sometimes it is claimed that it is the heart of Japanese culture. Understanding this helps it flower into life. The phrase itself arose from two separate words that were later put together.

Sabi

Japanese readers of literature first used the word *sabi* to try to describe the muted and subtle beauty of twelfth- and thirteenth-century poetry, with its autumnal feel and somber mood. The word has a melancholy ache to it, conjuring up rural images of faded and wobbly fence lines, fallow fields, and brown sparrows searching for food among crumpled autumn leaves.

Wabi

Wabi means poverty, but a genteel poverty such as is found in farmhouses where the family enjoys the riches of conversation and connection, while eating simple food from a simple hearth.

Wabi is the detachment from wealth, the recognition that money can't buy everything, and that it often buys trouble. Wabi is the resolved attitude of acceptance in the face of hardship and fear. We fear losing our job, or losing our spouse, or losing prized possessions, or losing talents, or losing our reputation. Wabi names the fear itself as the real difficulty and refuses to let it spoil life. It looks past want to what is essential for life.

Wabi was developed as a concept in the fifteenth and sixteenth centuries to tone down aristocratic tea parties. The gatherings were made simpler and simpler in order to emphasize the relationships and the gentle pleasure of simple communion.

Wabi sabi

When the two related terms were brought together into the phrase *wabi sabi*, it was a sign of humble grace. It describes a certain type of simplicity, not the simplicity of square apartment buildings, nor the unimaginative simplicity of mass media, mass transportation, or mass marketing. It is not about volume or size. Bigger is not better and faster is not fantastic. It is about travel at a human speed, eating natural food, and slowing down to be mindful. It is about respectful conversation, harmonious and peaceful dwellings, and modest behavior. It is ordered but not orderly, planned but not scheduled, simple but not simple-minded, and deliberate without being rigid.

In Japan it's had a lasting influence on literature, gardening, house design, and cooking. For those who choose to name it in their lives, to bring it out of its secret wordless place, it will grow strong and natural and the fruit of its branches will nourish the mind and soul.

I have it on good authority that there are no books in Japan that try to explain wabi sabi. The concept is an integral part of Japanese culture, but like the secret passed on to me from my father and grandfather, it is not part of the rational world. A largely intuitive concept, it is transmitted through example and only occasionally talked about. Historically it was the tea masters and Zen priests and monks who understood it. They understood that words can say too much and not enough about a subject that is so subtle and many hued. They also understood that, like Zen itself, wabi sabi was not something to be grasped by the intellect. Part of its delight is the mysterious difficulty we have in finding words to describe it.

Perhaps this is why it has fallen to individuals outside of Japan to try to put into words its essence. Taking this into account you will understand that the definitions and examples given here are meant to stimulate your own investigation into the mystery of wabi sabi through direct experience of it. The full expanse of wabi sabi cannot be grasped easily. But to help make the subject accessible, some rough distinctions can be made.

The inside and the outside

First, it is necessary to look at wabi sabi inside and out. Wabi sabi is a quality found in objects and nature. This is the outside we see, feel, hear, touch, and taste. This is the part that triggers emotions of longing, joy, loneliness, and contentment. This is what people are referring to when they say, "You can't explain wabi sabi; you just have to feel it."

The other part is the inside, or attitude. Wabi sabi attitude allows you to see and release your dependence on material possessions. It doesn't deny your needs but helps you discern the difference between needs and wants and the random desires you have picked up from others. With a wabi sabi attitude you can let the excess go, let things find their own place and pace, and allow the world to unfold as it does without having to control it. It is the presence of mind to enjoy the journey. It is about chosen poverty, but poverty that is a lack of clutter and an abundance of meaning. It is a life stripped down to what is valuable. It is not living without, but living within. It is a poverty that surpasses being rich, because it is mature, fully extended, balanced, centered, and aware. It is stillness of perception in a world of motion. It is about knowing what is real and lasting and also knowing what is transitory and fleeting, and knowing which of these things to focus on. It is being content with the simple things in life—content with everyday events, because they are lived fully. Really tasting, really seeing, really hearing, really being.

Wabi sabi, if fully realized, is a way of life. It may be helpful to contrast it with what is slick and stylish and plastic and faux. It

doesn't mean we don't use or appreciate all the positive techno-
logical advances of the modern world, but it does mean that we
understand the need to balance tech slick with wabi sabi.

The following chart will help clarify the essential differences
between wabi sabi and tech slick.

WABI SABI	TECH SLICK
NATURE FOCUSED	TECHNOLOGY FOCUSED
AUTHENTIC	COPIED
ALLOWS THINGS TO AGE	STRIVES FOR ETERNAL YOUTH
SUBTLETIES	BOLD AND OBVIOUS
INTUITIVE	RATIONAL
PERSONAL	IMPERSONAL
ONE-OF-A-KIND	CONFORMITY AND SAMENESS
IN THE MOMENT	FUTURE ORIENTED
THE WHOLE	SEPARATED INTO PARTS
OPEN AND UNRESOLVED	WORKS TOWARD CLOSURE
APPRECIATION	DEPRECIATION
SEASONAL	QUARTERLY
FLEXIBILITY	STABILITY
TOLERATES AMBIGUITY AND CONTRADICTION	INTOLERANT OF CONTRADIC-TIONS AND AMBIGUITY
PARADOXICAL	BLACK AND WHITE
UNREFINED	REFINED
ELEGANT	ORNATE
FRACTAL	SQUARE AND MEASURED
ORGANIC	GEOMETRIC

WABI SABI	TECH SLICK
LIVING	ARTIFICIAL
HANDCRAFTED	MASS-PRODUCED
SOFT EDGES	HARD EDGES
PATINA	PLASTIC
STONE	STEEL
LISTENS	TALKS
SEES	SHOWS
RECEPTIVE	ARROGANT
SLOW	FAST
HUMBLE	PROUD
PLAIN	FANCY
REFLECTIVE	UNCONSCIOUS
MINDFUL	MINDLESS
HEARTFELT	HEARTLESS
WARM	COLD

Two
What wabi sabi is not

trail to the lake

eager kids thunder past

trembling blue flowers

A FRIEND AND I KAYAKED on a July evening across Northumberland Channel to De Courcy Island just before sunset. The warm golden glow of the sun, low near the horizon, cast elongated shadows along the curving surfaces of the island's weathered sandstone cliffs. A bald eagle soared along the fir- and arbutus-covered ridge at the top of the bluff. We paddled slowly around each bend of the island's varied coastline and craned our necks to look up at the sculpted cookie dough shapes. When we pulled the craft in close, mottled rock, twisted trees, and barnacle-covered stones radiated the day's heat toward us, mirroring the warmth we felt at being there. We agreed to return on another night with our cameras to try to capture the weatherworn beauty.

True to our word, several weeks later we returned with our cameras, just as the sun was again setting behind us. For twenty giddy minutes we each snapped off picture after picture and then turned to watch the sun wink its brilliance out behind the distant hills of Vancouver Island. We were left to the evening twilight that melts all things visible into shades of gray.

In the moments after the sunset, our cameras stowed away, I noticed beneath my excitement a different emotion, unnamed and remote. It wasn't until days later that I was able to name it as disappointment.

When we had bobbed on the ocean that first night, our eyes scanned across the sandstone shapes exploring the visual textures as one great expanse. Each knob and hollow was connected by curving stone to other features, and in places the undercut created by the erosive action of the ocean made it appear as if the rock itself were a stony wave, suspended at its crest. On the second visit, however, peering through the camera's lens, the cliff face flattened and dissolved into abstract areas of geologic form. I could not take a picture of what my eyes and brain knew was there. The truth is that when we look about at the world, we see more than an accumulation of ordered images; we see beyond what can be caught on grains of photographic paper, beyond pixels or bytes, we see all the details together in one great visual gulp. On the first night I had seen each area of coast bathed in the memory of the rest of the island. The direction of the wind oriented my face, and bubbles popped along the barnacles as waves negotiated the creviced wall. All this informed my perception that we were in a place of flow, surrounded by tides and the great extension of ocean and air. We experienced the beauty in the movement of the boat and in the context of friendship, discovery, and shared appreciation of something indescribable, existing free and unencumbered by commentary or admission charges.

The images we gathered, on the other hand, are lovely little snapshots that show bits of the whole experience in square pictures of isolated sections of stone. The straw-colored grass tufts we paddled past revealed the depth of the shelves upon which they grew. But in the photographs they appeared stationary and blended to their background. Our attempt to capture the beauty we had experienced was only partially successful. The pictures were records of the light bouncing off a given section of stone at a given time of day, and records can never be the experience they record. We copy wabi sabi with cameras or sketchpads or tape recorders, or we try to re-create it in our home or office or yard. We want to experience the beauty again and again. My attempt to bring the stone cliffs of De Courcy Island home with me reveal a desire to hold on to wabi sabi beauty. But my experience showed the limitations of this attempt. Nature is always in motion, even rock, and any attempt to archive it, or arrest it for all time, ends up preserving only the desire, not the thing itself. Finally I began to understand something else. Copies change the original.

Buying wabi sabi

What happens when you make a copy or, worse, a copy of a copy? Pretty soon the end product of all the copying loses some or all of the appeal of the original. And more important, the original, by virtue of being copied, loses its uniqueness. This is the danger of manufactured items; the manufacturing process often compromises the copies. The end product can be very different from the original while still retaining its resemblance.

This is why original creations of art are so valuable. There is something in an original, when it is truly great, that is difficult to copy. Most of the time, the difficulty of reproduction is around the matter of subtlety. Paint on a canvas is lumpy and full of different plains, and the pigment reacts to the light in different ways, depending on the angle. There are edges to the brush strokes, and the canvas itself brings a quality to the painting. There is abundant evidence of the artist's hand.

When it is photographed and reproduced on a press, the color is a blend of dots or a blend of ink. It is an approximation of the original, and something is lost. Yet good prints of original paintings are still beautiful and worthy of display. But when you imagine a work of art reduced to a square the size of a postcard or wrapped around the edge of a facial tissue box, the effect changes, and while still attractive, it borders on something else. We now fill our houses with these low-quality images, and instead of capturing the beauty of the original they become part of the general blur and jumble. This is the culture of excess. There is now such a glut of images on cereal boxes, CD cases, knick-knacks, newspapers, magazines, and paperbacks, and all the inexpensive ornaments we collect, we are in danger of drowning in a sea of eye-catching design.

Can any of us find wabi sabi at the mall? Here are some preliminary suggestions on how to become a wabi sabi consumer.

Avoid temptation

First, if you have it within you, get rid of cable television. If you can't get rid of it, be aware that it is the single most effective way advertisers know to get you to buy the things you don't need. If you can avoid seeing new products, or seeing some star using or wearing these products, you will not be as likely to buy them.

Second, don't go shopping unless you have to. Simply seeing other people buying things subconsciously triggers you to buy things, too. Think about when you have hiked to the top of a mountain to have a look at the scenery. Do you think, looking out over that great vista, about buying a new penholder?

New research suggests that the decision to act is made long before you think you are deciding. By stripping your home and office of catalogs, flyers, and other advertisements, you pre-emptively avoid the unconscious lure of the new and improved. When people are bragging about their new car, or other desirable object, remind yourself that you are in control of what you buy and are committed to being a wabi sabi consumer. You are not your car, or anything else you own. It isn't owning that's important.

Find your Velveteen Rabbits

When some new item tempts you, remember the story of the Velveteen Rabbit. In the plethora of toys in a child's room, Velveteen Rabbit learned from the old Skin Horse that what makes a toy real is being loved. Skin Horse had all his hair loved off, but he explained to Velveteen Rabbit that this made him real; he had the ongoing attention of the child. The Skin Horse is wabi sabi. And while it is not his wabi sabi quality that endeared him to the child, the child made him wabi sabi with his love. As you begin to examine your own mass of possessions, ask yourself, "What are the Velveteen Rabbits in my life?" They might be a few special books on a bookcase full of less important titles. Give away or sell the less important ones and enjoy the old favorites again.

There is a tendency to fill our mantels with the pictures of our loved ones. Yet amassed together the jumble of frames and images are less evocative than a few chosen photographs. You don't need to get rid of the others; store them in a closet and rotate them several times a year. That way you will actually look at them, instead of letting them fade into the background clutter. Japanese homes sometimes have a separate storage building called a *kura* to contain boxes of family treasures that are brought out and displayed as the seasons change. The extra time spent organizing the items to be rotated pays off in renewed pleasure on seeing an item that has been in storage for a while.

If you go through all the stuff you have and give away or sell what you really don't need, you will be ready to open your life to new objects of beauty. No matter how wabi sabi an item may be, if it enters your life only to become part of the general background chaos, better to leave it on the store shelf.

When you are drawn to some wabi sabi item in the store window, ask yourself if it will bring you in contact with the natural world, with the changing of the seasons, or with the ebb and flow of the cycles and stages of life. Consider if there is a spot for it and what you are willing to part with in order to allow this item to fill a chosen place in your house or life. Remember, everything that is kept must have a keeper. If you don't want to dust it, or clean it, or oil it, or move it, or refill it, or empty it, or store it, or repair it, think hard before buying it.

Five ways people miss wabi sabi

It is easy to miss wabi sabi, often just because it is subtle, fragile, and understated. Here are a few things to watch out for:

1. Overcommitting to activities, no matter how worthy
2. Conforming against your better judgment
3. Focusing too much on the future or the past
4. Working for completion
5. Looking for the perfect solution

Overcommitment

Over time, we accumulate possessions, relationships, interests, extracurricular and after-hours duties, volunteer time, hobbies, social obligations, and even vacation expectations. Together they add up to overcommitment. Rather than letting any of these things go, releasing them for later enjoyment, we pick up new calendars, planners, and a Palm Pilot so that we can fit it all together. And our Palm Pilot acts like an accelerator, forcing us to pick up speed to keep up with all our commitments. Life seems too good to miss, and technology can help manage every moment. But at some point we realize we are missing moments, no matter how carefully we partition our schedules. We are missing lots of them, and the ones we are catching seem less and less meaningful.

We don't benefit from too much of any good thing; otherwise it becomes exactly what we don't want it to be. We need to specify for ourselves what is enough. But the lesson is not learned easily. We belly up to the smorgasbord or the buffet and our eyes grow wide and we take too much. We leave the smorg gorged and shuffle out with that distinctive waddle, belts bulging, chests puffing, and eyes rolling. Too much food leads to overeating, and too many commitments lead to obese days.

According to personality theorists, this overcommitted lifestyle is enjoyable for up to a quarter of the population. This quarter thrives on highly stuffed lives and looks forward to piling on new challenges and new excitement. Cell phones, e-mail, and laptops are efficient ways for these folks to manage the information inherent in such busy schedules, and they ratchet up the pace with the lever of ambition.

A number of years ago I was living this way. In fact, I was so busy that I exacerbated a stress-related illness and developed palpitations, panic attacks, and hyperventilation syndrome. To relieve some of the stress, I walked most mornings for forty-five minutes through a park near our house.

One morning while passing a certain spot on the path, I looked through a gap in the trees to where the sunlight was sparkling on a lake. The flashes of light caused by the gentle riffle reminded me of the complex flashes of light seen on the computer displays in old science fiction movies. I wondered if these apparently random flashes might actually contain a code that would reveal its meaning to the patient observer. I stopped in my tracks and stared at the flashing display for several minutes to see if I could discern a pattern. I threw my eyes slightly out of focus to see if that would help. The flashes illuminated the undersides of the leaves and glanced into the forest all around me. It was quite lovely, but no pattern or message emerged.

As I was turning to continue walking, I got a strange and sparkling feeling that opened into an inner message: "Trust the beauty." And after taking a few more steps, the inner glow revealed, "It's all going to change." I stopped walking and looked back toward the flashing ripples, but they were now hidden behind the foliage. I pricked up my ears and noticed that the forest was quiet around me, hushed even of bird song. It was as if some pivot had been reached and I was rocking around it to start a new direction in my life.

After my experience, nothing happened right away. I continued working and living at a breakneck pace and began to complain about how busy I was. I looked for a different job, hoping to find more money and less stress, the irrational hopes of a desperate man. Bouts of depression now interrupted my anxiety because I felt trapped by financial obligations.

Finally, through the help of family and a wise friend, I realized that I needed to make a change. The way of change was not readily apparent, but I looked for beauty and allowed the change to come. It arrived a year later, and I took a new job more suited to my personality.

If you are struggling in an overcommitted or overworked life and if you feel far from beauty and far from wabi sabi, talk to your family and friends and seek their advice. Sometimes giving up the fast lane and letting the speed demons race on ahead is the best way to find the balance that is right for you. Other options might include job-sharing or a renegotiated work schedule.

Wabi sabi cannot endure under an onslaught of stimulants and stress hormones; it will grow inside you as you let go of the commitments that are not essential and focus on what is.

Conformity

Wabi sabi is being authentic and mindful of your actions. Some people are blessed with this temperament from birth. Others long for authenticity but feel that the rules of business only work if you behave a certain way. So, large portions of the population play the roles they think are called for, all the while dehydrating their inner lives in hopes that at some future time they will be able to reconstitute themselves with the waters of achievement. The trouble is that playing a role you think you should only reinforces the role itself. It does nothing to realize the passion or purpose that is uniquely your own. This fabric of "shoulds" we end up wearing is like a garment of gold, appearing impressive to others but heavy and uncomfortable to wear. Find your passion and follow it if you can. Conform to your natural talents and abilities, instead of the expectations of others; then wabi sabi can develop in your work, friendships, and home.

Life out of focus

In Christian theology there is the expectation that a 1,000-year period will be related to the arrival of the Kingdom of God on Earth. Christians make a big deal about this and spend a lot of time debating over whether Jesus will return before or after the Millennium. People love to debate the future.

At the same time, Christians are waging a battle over our beginnings. Central to conservative Christianity is the belief that all that is wrong with the world came about because of the actions of Adam and Eve in the Garden of Eden. This is one of the reasons conservative Christians reject evolution and its conclusions about the development of our species. As long as people concentrate on the past or the future, they do not need to be overly concerned with the present.

Wabi sabi breaks out of this box of doctrinal dichotomy and asserts only this: All things are incomplete. Everything is motion. We cannot know for sure anything but this moment. We can be prudent in our planning for the future and we can reflect upon the events of the past, but it is in the present that most people find the reality of God, moving mysteriously in and out of time, transcending their limited view, and moving to release power into their lives, like rain into the soil of a garden. We have the opportunity to be blooming flowers moving between our beginning as a seed and our decay as fruit. Only by shifting our focus off the seeds and fruit will we see the sun that gives us life each day.

Working for completion

Much as you might like to, you cannot dissect wabi sabi and find its heart. Nor can you construct enough wabi sabi elements in your life to ignite an overnight transformation. Wabi sabi is not about parts, pieces, positions, or locations. It is not the sum of numerous wabi sabi digits added together to total a whole. One wabi sabi object can transform a room, if the nonessentials have been freed. But remember, wabi sabi is by nature incomplete. Your home will never be a finished masterpiece of wabi sabi decor, your work will never be completely done, and your life purpose will never be completely finished. If you think you have finished, you have moved outside of wabi sabi. What you can hope for is approximation. Warm closeness to the mark. Ballpark vicinity to the general feeling. You will find that both the inside and outside of wabi sabi are gradated. You can slide closer and closer without ever arriving. This is the sober side of wabi sabi. This is the side that makes people lose motivation and settle for imitations.

The most common imitation is wabi sloppy. Wearing that old T-shirt with the 2-inch holes, letting the grass evolve in the front yard so that neighborhood cats resemble tigers prowling the savanna, or never washing your car because dirt is, after all, very earthy. This is just being sloppy. It is not wabi sabi. In fact, it is quite the opposite. Wabi sabi is in the effort of an endeavor more than its final product. See what you can do during the life of a project and enjoy doing it. This does not mean there will not be order in the world, or that order is bad—only that all orders change. The old order often resists change and this is where wabi sabi can help. It can allow you to accept change and deal with it lightly because you realize that who you are and who other people are at any given moment is not who you and they have to remain, and the way things are now will not last forever.

Contrary to what is often thought, we do not work to change things as much as we work to keep things the same. If you release your control over events and people, you may find that a pattern emerges by itself. It happens in the forest and the field, so why not in your daily life as well?

What nature shows us is flexibility. Once while hiking in the Purcell Mountains, I came upon a grove of mountain willow blocking my path. The hike around the grove seemed long and arduous, so I decided to make my way through the middle instead. Dozens of thumb-sized and broom-handle-sized branches emanating from a central spot formed an upturned brush of foliage through which I attempted to travel. These gray-barked shrubs resemble weeping willows turned upside down. Any backwoods hiker who has tried to fight his or her way through a mountain willow grove will know that the springy trunks and branches are almost impossible to get through, because they bend and bend and will not break. They find their way into the folds in your clothes, the loops in your pack, the cuffs of your trousers, and gently push you away. If you are fortunate enough to make your way through a grove, exhausted, sweaty, and wounded, when you look back, you will find that your passage has gone unmarked. All the branches look as they did before. They moved out of your way when you pushed hard enough on them, with flexibility adapted to lying under a winter's worth of snow, and moved right back when you let go, as they do in the spring. Mountain willows demonstrate the virtue of being wabi sabi.

The perfect solution

When you decide to simplify your life, throwing off the heavy trappings that have collected like coats on the bed at a party; when you step out of the race against and toward the mindset that drives you past action to distraction; when you take the friction from your inevitable movement along the wall of life; when you let the continent of belongings shed you like a river, and you bring your lone attention to the shore of wabi sabi, remember, at its heart it is imperfect. And it proclaims in understated firmness that nothing is perfect. There is not a solution that will save you, or even salve you, unless you make the journey that is stillness. There is no solution to the busyness of life. There is only the decision to change how you see it moment by moment.

This is what wabi sabi can do for you. It can refocus your attention, rebalance your inner scales, and give you the gift of noticed change. Unwrapping that gift is a daily process, difficult and different each time. It is not an easy add-on. It is not a simple makeover. It is not a formula for success or a panacea. Like an action without movement, it beguiles you with paradoxes. Once glimpsed, it haunts you, and like a destination of memory it surprises you with its forgotten details.

I grew up in the small town of Nelson, British Columbia. A heritage site, its rough edges were restored over time by the residents who understood the importance of history to commerce. During my teens, the garish façades of the '60s were removed, and the original stone and wood walls were restored or painted. The restoration work made the town better than it had been, imparting oldness even to newly planted trees. When I left at age twenty-two, with my tentative ambitions, I was looking ahead, looking toward bigger and better things. And as my life inflated, my memory of home did too.

As I grew older, my reminiscences grew younger until my childhood home was detailed in exquisite light, each blade of grass sharp and covered with dew. It was as if all the details of growing up were magnified and lovingly preserved larger than life, so that when I did return there was always a brief shock of disappointment. "Is this really the same place?" I would blink. It seemed smaller. The mountains seemed higher and closer, and the streets seemed shorter and more ragged. I could not find the exact locations of things. It was good to be home, but home had moved, changed, and shifted.

I would return to my busy life, and over time my memories dried a little, shrank to normal. And in so doing they lost color, became blurred and faded like old photos. Then, during one trip to Nelson, I found that it was unexpectedly different again. This time I had underestimated it, shriveled it to avoid disappointment. Instead of just the place, I now noticed the colors, the people, the relationships, and all at once I was filled with longing to be there, to have what I didn't have. I thought if I could just return, just slip back into those lovely patterns of existence, everything would be all right. Sitting in a restaurant on Baker Street, watching the young granola-eating environmentalists around us reveling in their young culture, my wife Marilyn and I were pleased to discover that our children wanted to live there too. They were old enough now to appreciate the lake, the woods, the streams, the character of the town, the old hippies and young activists. We all saw how interesting it was. We were sad that we had to return to the place we lived and face not living in Nelson. But after the sadness faded we found we could visit Nelson as it was, appreciating its unique culture without needing to make it something it was not. Nelson is not perfect, but it is interesting and unique. Even a town can be wabi sabi.

Mass production, control, and artificial flavors

Our economy is based on mass production. I contemplated this while bird watching one late summer afternoon near our home. Sitting in the forest, camera in hand, I wondered just how the camera I was holding was made. How was the lens ground, where were the electronics manufactured, where did the factory stand that produced the enamel-covered brass casing? Did the manufacturing plants that make these things pollute the environment and take advantage of people in developing nations? In my sun-dappled woodland glade there was no sign of industry or commerce, yet in my hands was a precision instrument demonstrating all the virtues of technology and free enterprise. Anyone interested in wabi sabi can learn to live with the role that manufacturing plays in producing the things we use. Just because you are committed to wabi sabi does not mean you have to make do with old tools and equipment. It does mean, however, that if you like the old tools and equipment, you don't have to rush out and buy new ones. When you do need a new tool, just bring to mind the culture of excess, and let its true cost inform your decision. Commerce and trade exist not just to supply us with the products we need, but also to produce wealth for shareholders, owners, and investors. The profit motive, while effective at motivating work and competition, also encourages people to overlook other values like those contained in wabi sabi. Wabi can be interpreted to mean poverty, but it is a chosen poverty, not one imposed by circumstances or by those who hold the reins of power. And industriousness is needed if you are serious about this new way of life. You must actively examine the things you buy and the reasons you are buying them.

For wabi sabi to flow in your life you must find the balance between chosen action and chosen inaction. It is tempting to think that wabi sabi is phlegmatic, subdued, and inactive. This is partly because enthusiasts point to chairs and bowls and old wicker baskets—static objects that are not moving. But actually wabi sabi affirms the reality that everything is in motion, even the rocks that erode and re-form over millions of years.

There is a famous Japanese story about Takeno Jo-o and his disciple Sen no Rikyu that illustrates the role of effort in the creation of wabi sabi. The story illustrates how the principle of imperfection produces wabi sabi, but it has another message.

The young Rikyu was eager to learn the many rules and steps involved in the tea ceremony. As a test Jo-o set Rikyu to work in his garden, raking and cleaning and setting things in order. Jo-o would peek through bamboo blinds to observe the eager youth bustling about the grounds. He needed to know if this young student had the necessary intuition to come under his tutelage. When the work was done, Rikyu stood looking at his efforts. Everything was neat and tidy but something wasn't quite right. On an impulse of clarity, Rikyu ran to a cherry tree and shook it so that some leaves (or blossoms, depending on the version) fell randomly to the ground. Upon seeing this, Jo-o accepted Rikyu's request and taught him the way of tea. Rikyu went on to be the most important figure in the development of the idea of wabi sabi, so much so that authors on the subject of tea refer to pre-Rikyu and post-Rikyu to draw a distinction between the elaborate and richly adorned tea ceremony before his time and the simplified and wabi sabi ceremony after his time.

Notice that underlying this story's obvious message about the value of imperfection is a hidden one. The garden needed tending. Wabi sabi can be nurtured, and it can even be hard work. When creating a garden or handmade teacup, effort and control are necessary. The important thing is that the factors that impart wabi sabi be maintained. This is the danger of manufacturing. The goal of most manufacturing is to produce large quantities of uniform objects. This goes against the grain of wabi sabi. Subtlety and variability are lost. Mass-produced items appeal to the masses. Just as an appreciation for wabi sabi develops over time, so do the objects that embody it.

Most children love candy, soda pop, and potato chips. These products all contain bold, sometimes overwhelming, artificial flavors. Yet some of us, over time, grow to appreciate more complex flavors and the depth of taste we find in natural foods. Nutritionists and neurologists now know that children do develop their palate over time, and the process can be enjoyable and entertaining. If you have decided to simplify your life so that wabi sabi can develop strong roots, remember the enthusiasm and intuition of Rikyu and begin today to rake your life clean, and then shake a few leaves to make it wabi sabi.

Three
Wabi sabi
beginnings

every ten minutes

moving my lawn chair and book

back into the shade

THERE IS A STORY ABOUT A MAN who left his farm to seek advice from the Buddha.

"I'm a farmer," he said to the Buddha, "and I love farming. But last summer we had a drought and nearly starved, while this summer, we had too much rain and some of my crops did not do as well as I would have liked."

The Buddha, giving the man his full attention, nodded for him to continue.

"I'm married and she is a good woman. I love her, in fact, but sometimes she nags me and I get tired of her criticism."

The Buddha nodded with understanding.

"I've got three kids, too. They're great kids. I'm really proud of them. But sometimes they don't listen to me and don't pay me the respect I deserve."

The Buddha listened quietly. The farmer went on to explain in detail how his life was tainted by problems. Finally, he finished telling the Buddha all his troubles and waited for an answer that would set his life straight.

"I can't help you," the Buddha finally responded.

"What!" exclaimed the farmer. "I've heard that you are a great master. You have listened to all my problems and say you can't help me?"

"Well," the Buddha replied, "everyone has problems. In fact, everyone's got about eighty-three problems. Of course, you may fix one now and then, but another one will pop up in its place. If you think about it, everyone you know is going to pass away and all the things you care for will wear out or break. Your loved ones and your possessions are all impermanent. And you yourself are going to die someday. Now, there's a problem. What are you going to do about that?"

The farmer went red in the face and blinked his eyes in disbelief. "What kind of a teacher are you?" he sputtered. "How is this supposed to help me?"

"Well," the Buddha replied calmly, "perhaps I can help you with the eighty-fourth problem."

"The eighty-fourth problem. What's the eighty-fourth problem?" the farmer asked.

"That you want not to have any problems."

According to the Buddha there is only one law, and it is this: All things are impermanent. This law is at the heart of wabi sabi. The Buddha helped the farmer, not by solving his problems, but by showing him that the desire to be free from them is a problem itself. The farmer gained awareness when the Buddha set the problems within the context of the man's whole life and his certain death.

For most people wabi sabi begins in the eye, then moves to the "I." It begins as a love of something old or broken or almost broken. Sometimes it begins with seeing problems, and then seeing the desires associated with them. You will always have problems, and you will always have joyful times, but once wabi sabi becomes a part of your awareness, you will have perspective, that golden treasure that is so hard to explain. It will be on the edge of all you see, a reorienting clarity showing you the authentic life within the problems and joys.

This clarity brings depth to your perceptions. You will look out into the ramshackle world and appreciate the newness of puppies, the oldness of pagodas, the short life of chocolate cake and candles, the dimensions of grandmothers and grandmasters, the seasonal brevity of cherry blossoms and Halloween costumes. Seeing, just seeing, you will appreciate the bugs crawling at your feet and the satellites streaking the night sky. You will appreciate the wrinkled newborn babies and embrace the stunned new parents. You will smile when that young graduate takes her first step into the adult world, and rejoice in the newlywed's ardor.

And with the same clarity you will see wolverines and waste dumps, suffering children and panicked parents. You will smell the stench of corrupt officials, power-hungry politicians, and battle-weary soldiers. You will feel the deep loss of broken friendships, wasted potential, and declining social systems. The seasons will come and go, and you will ache with the clarity of knowing that life goes on, even while loved ones die.

In this funny way wabi sabi is just looking at objects and people as they move in and out of your view. Just looking, but a kind of looking that is an active verb, like a pig after truffles, rooting out the subtleties at work in your relationships with people and things. You will begin to see things down to the bone. You will roam across your own perceptions and harvest shades of meaning you hadn't noticed before. You will break out from your previously formed prejudices and sail both into and out of the patterns people make with their lives.

We humans love patterns; our brain finds them in clouds and tea leaves, and in the apparently random actions of others. Our language has patterns, our commerce has patterns, and our daily routines come and go with monthly regularity. But the thing about these patterns is that they are not exact. They weave around strange attractors, tracing similar orbits but never the exact same one. Do not be in a rush to see everything there is to see. Let it unfold naturally. Eventually what you see will change what you are. And then you will be seeing straight from your heart.

Becoming conscious of tattoos and logos

Skin can tell you things your mind cannot. Soft sensitive human skin covers you, covers your bones and organs and insides. Keeps your blood in; keeps you together. And then you lay over it clothes, allowing only parts of your skin to show, your hands and face. You protect your skin from the sun, from the elements—at least most of the time you do. At the beach, maybe, you will strip off your clothes, strip down to the minimum in swimwear. In that realm, near nakedness reminds you of your vulnerability, of how humans judge one another by appearance, of what is left when the dressing is removed. When people first meet, they see each other's face, hair, clothes, hands; they hear each other's voice, the parting of lips, and the rustle of cloth. They look at jewelry, watches, and rings. Summed up by possession.

At the beach the shape of your skin is able to speak again, after being locked away in cloth. Those who are aware of wabi sabi enjoy the beauty of young firm bodies but stray more often to the riot of folds and age spots and bushy hair that make up middle-aged bodies. Mortality is more evident in these frames. Medical alert bracelets dangle, scars show, cellulite puckers.

On the dwindling frame of calcium that slides away into the body quietly and ceaselessly, growing thinner and thinner while other tissues grow thicker and thicker, something else is happening. Like the stones in the depth of the crushing crust—melting in the mantle, being transformed by the pressure, eventually to be mined and milled—inside these aging humans precious stones are forming. They are the stones of character.

The teenagers at the beach are looking for the traces of smoke on the skin of their peers. These are bodies still in the fire, still hot and steaming. And along with the moles and birthmarks planted randomly across the young bodies, there are more recognizable shapes. These tracings, these patterns of choice, are tattoos. In the middle of the lower back, in the sacral area, these patterns lay. On shoulder blades they move, on biceps they bulge. Hidden during the pressure of the week, on the weekend they emerge, social signals that their owners have undergone the procedure, the rite of passage into the land of the bodily adorned. These young people have taken themselves out and been marked.

People receive marks for different reasons. Boxers wear casino logos on their backs while they fight, infuriating the "official" sponsors by garnering the casinos significant free advertising, which translates into actual activity at the casinos' Web sites. Bikers wear marks that tell other bikers who they are. The Japanese, whom we thank repeatedly for the concept of wabi sabi, were known to mark criminals with tattoos. In thirteenth-century Japan, the lopping off of ears and noses was replaced with a new, more humane way of marking a criminal. European countries tattooed their army deserters for many years, as well, and the United States, which tattooed its inmates with the name of the prison and their date of release, ended this practice in 1717.

I think about this while buying groceries. Around her arm the cashier has a weave of ink etched into her skin just below her shirtsleeve. Her arm moves back and forth, scanning the food. Her nametag says "Katie." Her straight hair is pulled back in a short ponytail. Her white company polo shirt displays a large store logo, a bright red blotch over her breast. Her employer has marked her with the company uniform. We see this as normal. We smile at the UPS courier in his brown uniform. This woman, tired and distracted, is not thinking about her status as a billboard for a grocery chain. She is not aware that I am looking at her tattoo, but for me the contrast is clear. One image she is required to wear by her employer, the other she wears out of choice.

Marking humans has never been widely accepted in the West, neither as a sign of ownership nor as a sign of individuality. It is painful and permanent. Tattooing in North America continues to be associated with rebels and outcasts. It is this association, no doubt, that explains part of the attraction for teens. The rebel has appeal, especially if he is the victim of unfair treatment. For the stage of peer bonding that typifies the adolescent experience, the appeal of the tattoo is strong. The marks are associated in our collective consciousness with questionable character. And this is the reason we feel uncomfortable when our children express interest in it.

But marks themselves can be wabi sabi. The patterns can be very old like the traditional patterns Polynesians now use to connect with their past. The coats of arms cherished by British families hold the same appeal. Other kinds of tattoos, created as one-of-a-kind emblems, can change the person who wears them, can permanently remind that person that he or she is different. We are makers of marks, be they the simple uniqueness of our signature or the intricate designs of our tattoos.

We love symbols, especially when they are old, carrying the weight of many years of use. Who can deny the appeal of the mark at the bottom of a Japanese watercolor painting made by a personalized stamp in red ink? Does the imprint on handcrafted pottery not carry the same appeal? Lovers of books often become lovers of fonts and other symbolic marks. We take a more or less arbitrary set of vocal sounds and use them to name things; then we take some visual symbols and attach them to the verbal sounds, and we have an alphabet. Then, we stylize the alphabet in a thousand different ways, and we have fonts. Then we incorporate certain characters of these stylized alphabets with simplified images and attach them to a cause, a company, a society, or a movement, and we have a logo.

For years I looked for a symbol to identify with. I was attracted to the cross, the fish, the snake eating its tail, the circle, the dragon, bamboo, $E=MC^2$, the galaxy, but none of them were appealing enough for me to want to engrave them in my flesh. The best symbols are simple and elegant but contain depth and history. When they are made of metal or bone or stone or fiber, they season and mellow over time into mottled objects of joy. Spare and basic, they communicate without words in primal and aesthetic ways.

Can a Nike Swoosh become wabi sabi? Not at this point in history, and not as long as it functions to sort people into those who can afford to buy Nike and those who can't. At the moment it is the opposite of wabi sabi, a subliminal device attempting to embed itself in our subconscious, stitching its form onto our brain. It is representative of all that is new, and kept new by the company. Old shoes are thrown out and replaced by new ones. Old shoes can, indeed, be wabi sabi, but shoe manufacturers are interested in selling you replacements, not celebrating wabi sabi. As well, there can be no humility in a name brand. Marketing is about saturation, self-aggrandizement, and sales. It is part of the culture of excess, the culture of conformity.

But things change. A number of years ago, New York youth began buying up the remaining stock of Hush Puppies because they were not cool; they were old and floppy and crepe-soled, and they were being discontinued. These youth were making a statement, choosing the unpopular, the frumpish, the grandfatherly. They were choosing wabi sabi.

When others followed, the company took note, and new Hush Puppies came rolling off the factory line again, but by then the original buyers were wearing something else. They did not want to be faddish; they wanted to be original. And that, perhaps, is how wabi sabi is maintained in a life.

Appreciation and the art of seeing

Thanksgiving, the "sweet as sweet potato" time of year when food and family surround us like snow surrounds a town, like bells surround us with sound, and where all the memories of childhood come back to us warm as firelight. We feel wabi sabi at Thanksgiving, perhaps more than any other time of year. The farms and fields are combed of grain and produce, the dormant ground appears as rich as potting soil, and the trees reveal their branchy bones and the wounds and marks of years of silviculture. Wood smoke is in the air and birds wing past on their way to far-off rain forests where fall never comes. Instead of that eternal summer, we in the temperate zone see the changes and transitions and progressions that spring and summer have left behind. When we pause to give thanks, we remember Thanksgivings past, we see the children, taller and older, jaws longer, eyes shrewder, laughter deeper, and we know that we, too, are older. Thanksgiving at its best is a time to do something we sometimes forget to do—appreciate what we have.

The practice of Naikan

Japanese culture takes the idea of Thanksgiving in a different direction. Almost universally people offer thanks before meals, and by so doing acknowledge our needs and the meeting of our needs with food and drink. But what if we took the candle flame of "saying grace" and used it to light a bigger fire?

Naikan is that fire. Naikan (pronounced "nye-kahn") is part meditation, part therapy, and part spiritual practice. And among other things, it is a good way to begin integrating wabi sabi into your everyday life, because it fosters humility, appreciation, and noticing.

Unlike our Western Thanksgiving, naikan is a quiet and private discipline that can be done by yourself on a daily basis, or with the assistance of a counselor or guide during a day-long exercise, or with a group at a retreat (sometimes lasting a week or more), or at a "naikan get-together" held at New Year's or on other important dates when deliberate reflection is valuable. The word means "inner observation," *nai* (inner or inside) *kan* (observation), and its secret is that it creates awareness through the simple act of remembering the significant people in your life.

Fifty years ago, Ishin Yoshimoto, a businessman and devout follower of the Jodo Shinshu way of Buddhism, was the first person to realize that the spiritual training given to Jodo Shinshu priests could benefit those outside the school.

Jodo Shinshu encourages love and self-sacrifice and emphasizes how these virtues were used by Buddha to help others achieve enlightenment. The training for the priests involves periods of fasting and meditation and other forms of self-deprivation. The idea is to see how food and the other necessities of life come as gifts from others, even when paid for. Food gives us more than the elements necessary to keep our bodies alive—it signifies love and care from the people around us.

Yoshimoto simplified the training of the priests and introduced it to the general public. So effective was it at reorienting individuals and helping them resolve their personal problems that doctors, nurses, therapists, and counselors took an interest. Now it is used with great success to treat addictions, depression, and truancy in youth. Sixty percent of the prison facilities in Japan have used naikan at one time or another. Prison officials report reduced rates of recidivism among prisoners who practice naikan, compared to others who are not following the naikan approach.

To gain the most benefit from this experience, you need to set aside a block of time and follow these instructions:

1. Find a quiet room.
2. Sit comfortably, preferably in a corner behind a screen with no other distractions.
3. Think about and/or write lists based on three questions.
   - What have I received from _____?
     (Name a relative, friend, coworker, etc.)
   - What have I given to this person?
   - What troubles, difficulties, or worries have I caused this person?

Think of and write down concrete examples such as, "My mother always made me a lunch before school and said she loved me as I left the house in the morning." General statements like "My mother was nice to me" just don't work.

Choose one person at a time and spend as much time as is necessary working through your history with that person from its beginning to now. Try to put yourself in the other person's shoes and feel what he or she has felt. When you have examined your three lists and are comfortable sharing them, talk to someone about it. At a day session or retreat a counselor or someone familiar with the method will regularly ask you, "What did you explore this time?"

By speaking aloud what you wrote, you will make it more real and confirm for yourself the importance of the process. Finally, when the time is right, express to the people on your lists your gratitude for the specific things they have given you. By doing this you will bring an authenticity to your relationship with them and reveal the wabi sabi nature of the gifts they have given you.

Radical wabi sabi and more realistic options

Early in our marriage, Marilyn and I moved fifteen minutes outside of Nelson to the farming district of Blewett, looking for a simpler life. This mountainside collection of farms and orchards rambles along the Kootenay River, as picturesque as any rural setting can be. Here we found for rent a log cabin, formerly inhabited by its owner, Mrs. Shoemaker, a widow who had farmed the land with her husband when he was alive. She had converted one of the chicken coops into a modest dwelling for herself so that she could rent out the "big house," the couple's original log house.

Everything seemed ideal for about two weeks, but then things began to go awry. Long-bodied mud wasps appeared like miniature helicopters throughout the house, and we discovered that the circa 1950 wallboard that was covering the upstairs bedroom walls hummed with the sound of untold numbers of wasps hidden somewhere behind the painted surface. Maggots began falling from cracks in the bathroom ceiling, so many that we resorted to brushing our teeth while holding an umbrella. The man at the hardware store raised his eyebrows and suggested that a rat or mouse had died in the ceiling and the rain of maggots would eventually come to an end. Shortly afterward the water quality began to change, growing first slightly yellow, then brown, then decreasing in pressure until there was no water at all. When Mrs. Shoemaker showed us the well, it was a circle of cinder blocks sunken in the middle of a cow pasture, into which we gazed with shocked silence. All that remained was sludge and mud drying and cracking at the very bottom. In my mind, at that very moment, the desert fathers, Francis of Assisi, Zen aesthetics, and the numerous other Thoreau-type back-to-the-landers wavered in the pantheon of simplicity and toppled down a rural well, never to be idolized again. I had realized with startling clarity that the simple life could get decidedly muddy.

It wasn't until many years later that I discovered a wabi sabi model that was less radical and more workable than pulling up stakes and moving to the country. The amateur astronomer John Dobson became my model.

Throughout the year, John Dobson and his fellow members of Sidewalk Astronomy unload homemade telescopes from the back of trucks and vans and then assemble them on street corners. The telescopes range in size from 3 to 12 feet tall and are made of a cardboard construction tube set on a plywood base. Society members hand-grind their two mirrors. Pointing the homemade scopes at the moon and planets, John and his friends invite passersby to look for themselves at our nearest neighbors in the sky, explaining to those who peep into the eyepiece just what they are seeing. John, a former Vedanta monk, is convivial as he reflects on his passion for public viewing of the universe. He explains that nothing beats seeing solar objects with your own warm human eye. And nothing motivates John to share his wonder more than the reward of seeing others glimpse for the first time those balls of gas and light that make up our galaxy.

I so admire that John constructs his scopes for very little cost and gives away the designs to those who want to make their own. His generous egalitarian spirit reflects the wabi sabi ideals of holding things lightly and experiencing the world directly. You may not be able to build a telescope and set it up on the street corner to share the wonder of the universe with others, but you can take the same attitude and look for your own unique form of living directly in the stream of giving.

Plain living as an alternative to living large

What John exemplifies is the realization that we don't need as much as we think we do to make our lives meaningful. Our desires for new and expensive things can blind us to the fact that in chasing after them, we give up opportunities to spend more time in direct contact with the world and the people in it.

A prosperous businessman once told me that the secret to being rich was just to think about money all the time. But who wants to think about money all the time? Cold, hard cash is definitely hard to earn and in the end it leaves like the air that leaves our lungs at death.

Wabi sabi breathes lighter air. It deals in "gander bills," the currency of seeing. It accepts the need for prudent management of financial affairs, but also sees the danger in excessive wealth.

Three hundred and fifty years ago Quakers called this danger "cumber," because they saw that the accumulation of material possessions impeded progress down the spiritual path. What was true then is still true—living large leads to debt, anxiety, and an overpreoccupation with money. In order to live spiritual lives within the culture of excess, Quakers developed a set of practices that balance and fortify a life of purpose. They called these practices Plain Living. There are many of these practices, and each was arrived at through personal experimentation. Here are a few that can be tried by almost anyone:

1. Clear-seeing
2. Freedom from deception
3. Questioning
4. Silence
5. Simple clothing

Clear-seeing

Quakers didn't start out embracing simplicity. They started out with an experience of direct connection to the Inner Light that illuminates every human being. They saw that all their daily activities should flow from what they experienced as true, that core of brilliant truth that centered them, and allowed them to see into the heart of things. They recognized that if their actions did not flow from this core of knowledge, then both the knowing and the doing were without value.

To keep their actions flowing from their inner clarity, they stripped away anything that got in the way. They called these things that got in the way superfluities and released them so that they could retain clear sight.

Freedom from deception

Quaker merchants are said to be the first to have set fixed prices on their goods. The conviction that all communication should be straightforward, without deception, rose out of their belief in honest speech. Bargaining cannot be done without holding something back, or without bluffing. In all our places of employment we can simplify matters by honest and forthright business. Never having to remember your deceptions frees up time for direct experience of life.

Questioning

Ask yourself questions. Pick ones that get at your values. "Does my feeling of self-worth come from my ability to earn money?" or "What am I avoiding today?" or "Did I trust my intuition or was I swayed by peer pressure?" By writing down and asking yourself probing questions, you stay true to your clear sight.

Silence

It is the source of all words. Out of it come thoughts, art, and every other human expression. Yet making time for it is difficult. Shared silence can be a powerful experience. In our world of talk radio, talk shows, discussion groups, political debates, and gossiping neighbors, many people have grown accustomed to the babble of speech and feel awkward with silence. But sometimes no answer is the best answer and a considered response is more valuable than quick wit. By making room for silence, and by using silence in your interactions with others, you will bring a needed depth to conversations. Rather than add to the blather, bragging, and bluster of others, encourage chosen words and chosen silence.

Simple clothing

There is nothing wrong with nice clothes. Once, a Quaker confessed to Mahatma Gandhi that he was overly attached to his collection of books. Gandhi remarked, "Then don't give them up. As long as you derive inner help and comfort from anything, you should keep it." Gandhi went on to explain that if you give up something in a mood of self-sacrifice or out of a stern sense of duty, and then continue to want the item back, such desires will make trouble for you. When you want to be free from the troubles of ownership, giving up possessions comes easy.

Clothing, unlike tattoos, can be changed, and you can say a lot with your clothes. Quakers adopted plain dress to emphasize their commitment to inner values of simplicity and to protest the use of slave labor to grow cotton. We can take similar actions today. Where are the clothes that you buy made, and how were the people who made them treated? Do your clothes draw attention to who you really are, or are they a disguise to make you appear something you are not? Do your clothes look and feel natural and support the values you espouse? Asking these questions helps to see that it is not the clothes that make the person; it is people who make clothes. We all have a choice in what image we will project with our garments. Wabi sabi clothes can be a mark of a natural and authentic style. We need not look plain or unattractive; wabi sabi is, after all, a kind of beauty—a beauty rooted in nature and balance. And when these qualities are sought in your clothes, they become a reflection of who you are, an authentic extension of your inner beauty.

Four
Wabi sabi
at home

bite mark on each slice

floppy buttered fresh cut bread

we chew together

BEGINNING, MIDDLE, AND END. Stories are a part of us, resonant patterns that shine out from our telling as we parse language with the twinkle in our eyes. Stories are birthed in words and shine with the polish of retelling. They unfold from our brains like language itself. Our thoughts form naturally into narratives that order our past like threads on a loom, woven together into the mystery of memory, sometimes incomplete, sometimes embellished, sometimes merely mended, sometimes just pure fantasy, imagination wrapped around a sequence. Some stories capture our experiences so well that we code them into text and seal them on paper or other paperlike media so that they can be preserved as history, or myth, or song, or epic poem, or reminiscence, or biography, or autobiography.

We talk and write and paint and sing and dance and dramatize our stories, making the heart known, or making the message clear, telling about us, the inner we, the self before ending, before we come to an end. This is the pleasant act of narration, the satisfaction of revealing some of our essence before it is gone. By doing this we release the fear that others might not hear this message we are conveying.

Around the evening meal, around the common table, our family has the habit of story. Each night we have the chance to tell and listen as conversation and plates are passed around, as steam and smells of food mix with images of one another's day.

We eat it up, this language stew, these delectable bits of news. Each person, old or young, has a view on the world and his or her own take on things. We listen and become authentic in the listening and the telling. Story exists in that thing called family, that thing that clearly embraces those with whom we share our lives. It wraps like a chord of music, like a vibration of emotion, between the bowls and dishes and utensils and objects touched and released—a salt shaker of words, a pepper grinder of ideas.

Family is a collective agreement to be connected, to share our stories and food. Communion glows like a halo over the ritual of eating, the choice to be together for this common need, this life sharing.

Telling stories and the family table

At our house we take a moment to say grace before our meals. In it we tell a sort of story: "Thank you God for the day, for the sunshine, and the friends we shared time with, thank you that we live in a country that is free and that we have a safe home, a caring family, and good food like this to enjoy. Bless our time together around this table. Amen."

Did you see it? Maybe just a glimpse? The sunshine, the friends, the food? Grace can set the stage for sharing; it can prime the pump of appreciation. We invite God to be a witness at our table, included in our time together.

A reservoir of deep myth over which our mind constructs a kind of fishing wharf underpins much of what we do in common as human creatures. From that wharf we fish out lessons from the depth. We do this naturally, and from the rolling mass of experiences, we shape the stories we tell to others. We make sense of our experiences through the application of the narrative device. Some stories are so good we tell them over and over, sometimes to the same people.

Memory has a tenuous function in this process at best. A story told from memory is often modified to such a degree that those around the table feel compelled to jump in and correct our misperceptions. "That is not how it was. The truck was almost stopped, and it was a bluish light, off to the west. We didn't even comment on it at the time."

When language is new

When our children were first learning language, we used a memory book to collect funny anecdotes and stories that surround that magical time of making novel speech. When they were a little older, the children loved to hear these stories about themselves.

When one son was three he was bored in the house and wanted some excitement. Marilyn took him out to ride his trike on the driveway, where there was a puddle from a recent rain. She told him he could jump in it if he wanted, and later in the house as they peeled off the wet pants, he exclaimed, "My pants are wet as a piece of bacon!"

After being a typical seven-year-old, one son was sent to his room for a time out. When Marilyn checked on him later, he started to sob, "I'm the worst. No one loves me. I think I will just kill myself."

"Oh Son," Marilyn said, "we love you very much, and you're not the worst. If you feel that way, perhaps you need to see a counselor."

"What I need," he retorted, "is a lawyer!"

At the time this incident actually happened, this child felt anger and sadness; but now, on retelling it as a story, he feels warmth and humor. Such is the wonder of story.

One son had mastered complex sentences and was very interested in stories. He liked it if I told him stories I made up on the spot. I would try to give the stories little morals. Soon we started taking turns; I would tell a story, and he would tell one back to me. At first the stories he told back to me were pretty much the same story I had just told him, but with cosmetic changes. Then one day when I was getting ready to go out for the evening, he wanted to tell me a story. We sat on the couch, and he began, "Once upon a time there was a leprechaun. He had long pink ears and looked like a rabbit." He paused and wrinkled his brow. "Actually," he confessed, "he was a rabbit." I started laughing, and he started laughing, and pretty soon the rest of the family came in, and they started laughing, and we never did get back to the rest of the story.

We have committed many of these anecdotes to memory now. They mark the passage of time, mark the seasons of life, and weave the sense of family again and again into that fabric of memory. They are not fancy or dramatic but they capture moments of humor and daily life. In retelling them we remind

ourselves that these events, small and domestic, are the stuff of
wabi sabi.

The simple pleasures of wholesome food

Stories and food seem to go together, and they reinforce wabi
sabi in our lives. In sharing these sabi things, these tales, thread-
bare and common, and in sharing traditional foods, familiar and
homey, we wrap ourselves in the unseen history of our own
authentic culture. Not the dramatic history of wars and conquest
and invention and industry and domination and exodus, though
we may tell those stories during meals too.

Wabi sabi is in the common, embarrassing, humorous stories,
the odd, wacky human stories, the stories that reveal our true
selves, our limping characters, and our faltering steps toward the
stage we are in now. And surrounding this, at the solid plane of
wood or tile we call the table, around these stories sit the
everyday items that allow us to continue, the nourishments that
enter our bodies and keep us alive, and the bowls and utensils we
use to prepare and eat that nourishment. The same things
brought out again and again, held in our hands over and over, forgotten in their familiarity.

Families have a vast repertoire of meals from which they can
choose, but on a week-by-week basis most have the same seven
to ten meals again and again. Every once in a while some
recipe, remembered or found, nudges out one of the others.
Familiar foods are wabi sabi because they are familiar, common,

unnoticed, but unfamiliar foods can be wabi sabi, too, because the first time we sample a new taste, it rushes at us with its unique flavor and holds our attention and reminds us of what eating is—the consumption of substances found in nature. By eating we introduce nature into ourselves.

The choices we make about what we eat will influence how we feel about our connection to that source from which all our life flows. If it has been processed, extracted, converted, or manipulated beyond recognition—like sugar is when it is spun into candy or soaked into soft drinks, or like dairy products are when they are turned into cheese spread, or like flour is when it is mixed into fried dough—then it no longer informs us of our connection to the land. It is just stuff, "fast food," because it allows us to stay fast and not slow down and savor our food, as a meal should do. And there is so much that food can tell us if we only take the time to listen.

Rice

Consider the rice plant. An annual related to grass, rice depends solely on being seedy for its propagation. Because of its unique ability to produce outrageous amounts of grains when half-drowned in water, it has become the staple food of about half the world's population. Humans eat more rice overall than any other single food. Why has rice risen to this status? The secret is in its genes.

Rice is a dry-land plant that evolved in areas of flood. Its seeds can germinate underwater in the sludge of a sunken field.

The seedling is adapted to seek out air from a considerable depth. Once it has established an above-water leaf or two, it sucks in air through pores and distributes it as a thin cushion around the underwater surfaces, stock and stem. This process accelerates when the plant starts producing carbon dioxide, which dissolves in water much more quickly than oxygen. The carbon dioxide is released into the water and the reduction in pressure draws in more air. Some species can elongate the stalks between their nodes at a rate of 10 inches a day, thus keeping their heads above any rising in the flood. Growing this way, a single rice plant can reach 16 feet. Special roots at the top of the plant grow so that if the swirling waters uproot the whole plant, it can gather nutrients from the water and float free until it touches bottom again as the flood recedes. This ability makes replanting easy and thinning becomes more a matter of spreading out than throwing out. Consequently very few plants are lost. Since the grains mature above water, they can be gathered by boat or, if the water has abated, on foot.

Rice now thrives from Egypt to Australia, Argentina to France—in fact, almost anywhere there are warm summers and water. Because the plant produces so prolifically in water, great effort is made to provide diked paddies. They must be almost level, with just a slight grade for water flow, and the dikes must be guarded from breakage.

Interestingly, a form of cooking developed in response to paddy construction around the fourth century B.C.E. Keeping the land flooded with water ensures that no other land plants can grow, but it leaves fuel in short supply. As a result, people learned to cook with small, hot fires that burned quickly, and woks were developed for this kind of cooking. Into the wok went finely chopped vegetables, eels, fish, frogs, edible rats, and dried oysters, so that the small pieces would cook quickly. The fried items were served over a steaming bed of, as you might expect, rice.

Because everything is chopped ahead of time and because chopsticks are used, wok cooking is sanitary and simple. This serving of cooked diced vegetables and meat over rice is so old that it is embedded in Chinese culture at a fundamental level. The diced topping is called *ts'ai*, which means "topping" or "flavoring," and the rice itself is called *fan,* a word synonymous with food in general. *Fan* is part of the ancient system of yang and yin. Of the five elements that make up the physical world (metal, wood, water, fire, and earth), *fan* is related to earth. *Ts'ai* is related to fire. Recognizing this and the connection to the earth that it brings can make each meal with rice an opportunity to acknowledge earth and fire, two elements of wabi sabi.

Consider cooking this way more often, so that you can see the vegetables and meat as you eat. Contemplate the way food exists in its raw form, and acknowledge that other things die so that you can live. This realization does not have to be maudlin. Many of the people who live close to the land, who plant and harvest and raise and butcher their own food, thank the plants and animals for this sacrifice. By doing the same thing you can connect to the chain of life at each meal.

Rice pudding is a good way to end any meal. The pudding recipes themselves range across the globe from the simple British brown sugar and cinnamon affair to the amazing Turkish concoction of vermicelli baked in honey. And for some reason this particular utilization of rice stimulates feelings of nostalgia in most people. Rice pudding has that warm domestic feel of so much that is slow-cooked. Each roll around the tongue triggers fond feelings from childhood. Each spoonful is a steaming reminder to slow down, savor the moment, and take time for the simple things. Each replumped raisin is an opportunity to explore texture and substance. The cinnamon imparts its earthy tones, making the whole experience a layered wabi sabi treat.

Bread

When you bake bread, you participate in a daily ritual common throughout the barren places around the Fertile Crescent. Humans have been eating wheat itself since it was first discovered sometime during the Paleolithic Age. In its dry kernel form, wheat keeps well and can be planted in the spring to ensure a new crop. No one has found an ancestor of wheat, which suggests that it has been cultivated for a very long time. Some estimates place its first cultivation in the Neolithic Period. Historians know for sure that the Egyptians learned to grow wheat along the Nile, and it became their staple food sometime between 30,000 and 5000 B.C.E.

Beer production occurred in Egypt around the same time, and it is conjectured that the knowledge of beer and wheat fermentation developed in tandem. One story tells of an Egyptian boy charged with baking the bread who fell asleep and let the fire go out. By the time he restarted the fire and baked the bread, the natural yeasts had done their work. Because of its high gluten content, wheat was the highest rising dough of all the grains available at the time and quickly became favored over oats, millet, rice, and barley.

The Egyptians also developed ovens in which several loaves of bread could be baked at the same time. Bread for the rich was made from wheat flour, bread for the middle class was made from barley, and bread for the poor was made from sorghum. The workers who built the pyramids were paid in bread, and the word *bread* is still slang for money.

By 3000 B.C.E., hardy strains had been selected, including kamut, which is still available for purchase today. Bakers regularly fermented their flour and water mixture using wild yeasts that were present on the grains and in the air. These wild yeasts are still present, and you can make a delicious loaf the same way the ancient Egyptian bakers did.

There is a form of bread making that is almost as old and much more interesting to behold. The bread produced is called natural-rise bread; I have come to call it Wabi Sabi Bread.

Wabi Sabi Bread: the recipe

Take 2 cups of lukewarm spring water, and add 1½ teaspoons sea salt and 2 tablespoons of olive or sesame oil. Gradually add, 1 cup at a time, 5¾ cups of stone-ground or home-ground whole-wheat bread flour until the dough becomes dry and firm.

Turn the dough out onto a floured surface and allow it to rest for a few minutes. Knead the dough by hand until it is smooth and resilient. Wabi sabi dough requires more time to knead than other doughs. Use a bread hook in a food processor if you are unable to knead by hand, but enjoy the smell of the fresh dough and the feel of its rounded surface.

When the dough is firm and elastic, form it into a ball and place it in a bowl greased with olive oil. Cover the bowl with a damp towel and a solid cover, like a flat plate, and set it in a draft-free spot for 40 hours. That's right, 40 hours! Yes, that is a long time, but trust me, it is worth it.

Don't think that it has to be warm to rise. A cool room is actually best, so that the biological agents work slowly. Take a look at the dough from time to time and knead it three or four times when you think about it. This presents different surfaces for the yeast to grow on. After each kneading, redamp the towel. You will notice when you knead it that the fragrance and feel of the dough will change, taking on a sweet smell first, then a slightly sour smell as well. And most remarkably, it will begin to rise, not as dramatically as yeasted white breads, but a noticeable amount.

After those 40 hours have gone by, turn the loaf out and give it a quick knead. It should be slightly spongy by now, but still soft and relaxed. Put it into a greased bread pan; it should fill about 2/3 of the pan. Lightly grease the top of the loaf and cover it with a damp towel. Let it rise for another 3 to 7 hours at room temperature. It should fill the whole pan.

Slash the top of the loaf and place it in a cold oven. Set the oven to 250° to 300° (not too hot), and bake for 1½ hours or until the bread is browned and slips easily from the pan. Let the bread cool completely before you cut into it.

Wabi Sabi Bread: tips and hints

Wabi Sabi Bread is more flavorful and moist than other whole-grain bread because of the long fermentation period. During that time, natural yeasts that are present on the surface of the grain grow and convert carbohydrates into sugar and acids. The biologically converted dough absorbs liquid thoroughly and produces a subtle fine-grained loaf with a natural sweetness and the aroma of sourdough bread.

This is not sourdough bread, as that term is generally understood. No sourdough starter is used—just the naturally occurring yeasts present on the grain. For this reason, organic whole grains work best. If you do not have your own flourmill, ask around; you may have a friend with a home flourmill. Barring that, you can purchase newly ground flour from a bakery or health food store.

The minerals in spring water facilitate fermentation, while chlorine and other chemicals in tap water can hamper it. So, with good quality water, you only need 2 cups. If you can't get spring water, filtered water will do.

Quality sea salt regulates the fermentation process and fends off unwanted organisms.

No two Wabi Sabi loaves are the same; each one is unique in flavor and shape. The finished crust is chewy and attractive and seals in moisture and flavor. In fact, if stored at room temperature,

Wabi Sabi Bread will reach its peak in flavor and texture two or three days after baking as its crust softens and the crumb mellows. You can slice it thinly and it will hold its shape. Eating it will be an opportunity to reflect on how time and patience often produce the best results in any endeavor.

Wabi Sabi Bread can benefit from the addition of booster ingredients that will speed up fermentation in a natural way. One simple change is to add miso (unpasteurized and containing the live enzymes) in place of the salt. Use 2 tablespoons of miso and a little more flour, maybe ½ cup. The natural enzymes help the dough change and become more nutritious.

The kernel of truth

The Christian communion service ponders the role of Jesus as spiritual sustenance. The ceremony is full of analogies. Dust (flour), water, and breath (yeast-created carbon dioxide) combine to make bread in the same way that God took dust and water and breathed into it to make humans. Jesus was born in Bethlehem, which means "the house of bread." In numerous parables, Jesus used grain and the work with grain to illustrate his teachings. He compared himself to bread and wished that his message would be internalized, as bread is when we eat it.

Like a grain of wheat that is buried in the ground, Jesus was buried and rose from the dead. On the night before he was to die, Jesus asked his friends to remember him when they sat down to eat. Every time bread is consumed, it is an opportunity for

Christians to ponder Jesus's words, which like good grain can take root in our lives and produce a bountiful crop.

Eggs and onions: wabi sabi symbols

Female reproductive cells. Several of them roll around inside a dish and their smooth white shells click each other with that threateningly thin sound that tells me to be careful, very careful, carrying these around. Most of the time sexual cells are kept private, on purpose, but these eggs are so commonplace they never make anyone blush, unless it is pointed out just what, in fact, they are.

I am ten years old in the St. Andrew's-by-the-Lake Anglican Church Hall, in the kitchen, and I have just stored my dish of secrets on a low shelf. I go and join my father, who is holding up one of the female reproductive cells in front of his class of Sunday school children.

He conceals it in his hand in such a way that only the round end shows between the curve of his thumb and the mirror curve of his fingers. "A white ball," he says, and the children nod, "but this ball is special. If I warm it to just the right temperature for just the right amount of time, it will turn into a bird." Shocked expressions appear on several of the children's faces. Magic? From their Sunday school teacher? My father peels up his fingers and rolls his hands around so that he presents to the class the naked chicken egg on the palm of his hand. Shock turns to knowing, and then to wonder. Some of the children will remember this revelation; things are not always what they seem. Knowledge changes knowing.

In the late summer, when the time is right, all the songbirds on Vancouver Island start to fly straight up, at night, toward the stars. All of them, mind you, do this at the same time. They keep flying as if they are heading for outer space until they hit the jet stream that snatches them like fluff and blows them south. You can see this on clear nights in August by looking at the full moon with binoculars. There, thousands of tiny specks race across the face of the moon: songbirds. And all of them hatched in little twiggy nests from mottled little eggs.

Wabi sabi begins as an egg, smooth and plain on the outside, and full of life on the inside. It is in plain view and not hard to find. It is a graceful curve as old as rain. It has been with us since we began, incubated over the centuries, ripened in the earth, and consumed without recognition.

Then, one day someone points to it and says, "You know, that is wabi sabi," and suddenly the shell that contains us breaks open and we lay in a swirl of feathers in the bottom of a nest, and see a sky full of stars, or full of one star that blots out all the rest.

It is then that we realize, staring up at the blazing egg in the sky, that in the rhythms of reproduction, in the cycle that curves around an individual, is this shell of beauty, containing the many moments that are a life: growing feathers and a hard point on its beak so that we can break out into the cold awareness that is this moment, this wabi sabi moment that reveals us, there in the mess, human after all, and still wet with wonder.

Part of wabi sabi is opening the shell of experience and seeing inside, feasting on the inner glow of life, but wabi sabi is more than the yolk, or the white, or the chick that eventually emerges; it is more than the bright yellow warbler that will race skyward on its wings in the liquid of flight at night for a waiting wind. Wabi sabi rests also in the emptiness, the freckled fragments left behind on the forest floor. For wabi sabi is often recognized in the thing left behind, the stage you move on from, the memory you recall fondly, and it tags these remnants with a little square label that says, "look, meaning."

The Israelites, during their long trek through the desert, remembered the food of Egypt, and while they had manna as a substitute for bread, finding a substitute for onions was harder. Not just because onions are wonderful food, but also because they represent the Egyptian universe. Round, layered, and concentric, the nine globes of large-celled translucent onions represent eternity and the wonder of creation. How does the onion know it should be round; does it mimic the globe in whose surface it grows? In the minds of those remembering its taste while they traveled through a dry desert, the onion held all the apparent wisdom of what they were leaving. Each layer of onion is designed so that as it dries, it protects the inner layers from the same fate. Break the outer skin and the inner onion is fresh and whole.

The onion we serve at our tables is the bulb of one of several varieties of plants all known for their odiferous and sulfur-based compounds. The bulb actually consists of fleshy leaves, called scales, which fold over one another in a tight ball underground to store and provide nutrients for the second year's flower. The flower, also globelike, is a grand display of symmetrical beauty perched atop a tall hollow stem. In this way the globe of the air mirrors the globe in the soil, lending itself to an analogy of the conscious mind in the brain mirroring the unconscious mind in the soul. The bulb, folded and compact in the dark soil, is connected by the stalk to the airy and beautiful flower in the same way that the soul, folded and compact in our own inner darkness, feeds the flower of our awareness. And while it is the flower that makes us smile, it is the bulb that makes us weep.

And this kind of weeping jolts us awake, serves to remind us that our noses can be useful tools in the cultivation of wabi sabi. The smell of good home cooking filling a house can remind us of the seasons of life. Onions are often a part of the slow cooking that signals winter, steamy windows, and hearty meals. It reminds us of the warmth that is inside, while outside it is cold and dark.

Fasting restores richness to your life

Many people give up certain foods at certain times of the year. Christians give up luxury foods for Lent, Muslims give up daytime eating for Ramadan, and Jewish people eliminate leavened products during Passover. As well as these major fasts, many religions and cultures prescribe fasting for periods of time every week. Yet individuals who grow up outside of these traditions often misunderstand this "going without" behavior.

These days, when people go without food, it is often because they have booked too many commitments into a day and literally cannot find time to eat. Unlike missing a meal for the sake of a schedule, fasting is a decision to go without food for a spiritual or humanitarian reason. We are in the habit of eating regularly and indiscriminately, and breaking this habit, from time to time, allows us to concentrate on what it means to be hungry and on any reason we have for going without. That reason may be to devote more time to prayer, or it might be as a symbolic elimination of an influence in our life, or as a gesture of solidarity with those less fortunate.

From a wabi sabi perspective, fasting can be an opportunity to observe the phenomenon of saturation, to see beyond the misconception that wealth allows an individual to have anything he or she wants. And people who experience windfalls often do rush out and buy the things they have always wanted. But after a certain period of time these folks must buy more things in order to remain happy with their wealth. This process of diminishing returns reveals that the act of purchasing nice things is pleasurable, but the reality of looking after lots of things is not.

A life saturated with belongings demonstrates that the same things that bring delight become burdensome when insurance costs rise, storage space is used up, and general clutter becomes annoying and unattractive.

In theory, given enough money, a person could keep buying bigger houses and more items to fill them. But there is a different way of enjoying life that does not require a bigger house. It is the wabi sabi way.

In our house, come December, we purchase ingredients to make several special treats we never make the rest of the year. Commemorating the cooling of the season, we serve two cold desserts—a whipped lemon-egg dessert and a layered chocolate dessert we call Nanaimo Bars. After our evening meals in December, with the rain or wind sounding against the windows, we slice the cool winter treats and savor their unique flavor. As with most foods, the first bite is always the best, and in that moment the time between years melts away, producing a pleasure of both taste and of memory. The unique flavors evoke the forgotten depth of time and tradition.

The recipes I use to create these treats are my mother's. Scottish and English coal miners arrived on Vancouver Island in 1854 following the discovery of coal in Nanaimo. A long way from home and burning a tremendous amount of calories in the cold wet mines, the hard-working men enjoyed a treat sent from England that later became known by the name of the city in which they lived. Butter, sugar, chocolate, vanilla, graham wafer crumbs, and coconut are not particularly wabi sabi ingredients, but because of this particular combination, and because they are only enjoyed once or twice a year, we appreciate them more than we would if they were a weekly food.

If you find that the things that used to give you pleasure (ornaments, clothes, games, sports equipment, etc.) have lost their appeal, or if food doesn't satisfy like it used to, take some time away from these things to allow your body and mind time to find a new baseline. Then, when you reintroduce your hobbies and possessions and that special food, you will experience them as something out of the ordinary, special, and pleasing.

Hanging clothes on the line and other deliberate acts of slowness

For us on the rainy West Coast, we cannot hang clothes on the line year round. Unlike my children, I love the feel of bath towels dried outside. They seem to be more absorbent and I enjoy the pleasant scratchiness that invigorates the nerves as it takes the water off my skin. I like the smell and texture of the towels, stiff and substantial. There is also something humble about drying clothes on the line.

Some exclusive neighborhoods do not allow outdoor clotheslines. They are seen as ugly and low class. For this reason, they are wonderfully wabi sabi. Flowerbeds and greenery surround our clothesline, making the work of putting out clothes more tolerable. In addition, the act of pinning my underwear and socks in the sunshine forces me to handle each item, and realize my need for clothing. At the same time I hang out the family's clothes, noticing how much bigger the kids' pants are this year, feeling the weight of the fabric and appreciating the variety of clothes we have to wear.

We can view time-consuming activities like this as just chores, annoying wasters of our time. But by looking at these menial chores of life as opportunities for reflection, we can then appreciate the free time we have once the chores are done.

In conversation recently with some men my age, we discovered that our fathers shared an endearing habit: letting the night fall. One friend described how his father took time after supper in the summers to sit quietly in the living room and let the night happen, let the sunlight fade off the trees, let the gray twilight usher in the little brown bats while he serenely watched the stars come out one at a time in the darkening sky. My friend has pleasant memories of his father sitting in the dark, content with simply being there.

My own father used to invite me to venture outside just before dusk to simply experience the beauty of the yard when all the edges were smoothed by the long angles of light and the coming darkness. We called it "cruising the yard," and it was a time of quiet observation and conversation as we allowed the world to revolve under us, taking us into night.

Unlike the onion, the electric light bulb has little to contribute to the wabi sabi way. It compels us to work longer hours, spend less time in natural light, and remain longer indoors. Most of the forms of entertainment that keep us from going outside involve the steady, unchanging glare of electric lights. We play computer games, watch TV, go to movies, shop in malls, and do office and house work under the steady hum of artificial light. Consider going on an electricity fast. Turn off the stereo, TV, and electric lights. Turn off the computers, printers, GameCube, and gadgets. Reconnect with the subtle pleasure of a day coming to an end naturally.

I have considered turning off the main breaker in the house from time to time, to simulate those occasions when the power goes out because of a storm or accident. It is when the juice is cut off that we realize just how much of our lives depends on that current of electrons traveling into our houses. But it doesn't have to be that way. If a full-fledged "electricity fast" is unworkable in your day, have a media fast. Don't even look at the news or listen to the radio. Enjoy silence and the relief of not having to hear more depressing news. Go to bed early and get up to watch the sun come up, and share these times with your family and friends. Tell them it was something your father enjoyed, or tell them you want to spend time with them. In these small ways you can introduce the natural rhythms of the seasons back into your life.

Five
Wabi sabi friends

mountain lake fishing

dad's thermos of orange pekoe

we share the lid-cup

TEA: CURLED, DRIED, RASPY BITS OF LEAF, withered, shrunken, dried, packaged. You need a lot of it to tip the scale, but it grows on trees, tea trees pruned into undulating blankets covering hillsides like a wrinkled brain. Mountains of tea in China, India, Korea, Thailand, Taiwan, Japan, where nimble hands prune, harvest, and fertilize. Money plants, shiny and green, with us, simply there, simply existing since way before humans knew, even guessed, that this bitter sharp leaf would become the most harvested leaf of all.

I love coffee, good coffee, made strong and rich. It, too, is bitter, no matter how you roast it, which makes it go so well with something sweet, like a Danish or slice of cheesecake. Coffee is blood to the masses, the necessary juice to slick tired veins, to rev glands, and keep a person facing what he or she otherwise couldn't face. Steel-like, bracing, it hits the body hard with acid, caffeine, taste. Gotta have it; gotta keep going. It fuels the panic, the controlled jitter at the heart of commerce, at the racing heart of industry.

The coffee break, not really a break to relax, not to unwind, not to rest, is meant to break the slide from productivity, break the wavering mind with black hot energy, and bring the system back online, on task, on target. Coffee sharpens the buzz, the bead, the clutching fear of falling behind; it puts an edge on people, hops them up. Coffee runs us, keeps us running. We love it because it supports the quickness we value, keeps us alert as a thorn, as a needle, pains us awake with sudden clarity.

Now feel tea. Those shriveled little leaves, lolling in the pot, unfurling like sails, swimming in the hot water, bleeding out their flavonols, their bound caffeine, their subtle phytochemicals. Polyphenols swim into the brew; catechins tumble in waves. Tea is gentle, delivering its caffeine slowly, and its taste is gentle, leafy, and fuzzy on the teeth. Tea rejuvenates, rehydrates, invigorates. Teatime. Midafternoon tea. Nothing hurried about it; civilized, elderly, advocated for sobriety. Tea is closer to perfume, wafting over us like tender rain, a mist of arboreal tone. Teacups, thin and fragile, flowered, with a saucer. Fluted, curved to meet our lips.

The teashop. Hear the bell on the door as we enter. Not an electronic chime, but a real brass bell on an ornate hook. Here is the owner; see her watch our nostrils flare. The teashop smells so good. "Oh it smells so good in here," we say. "That's what everyone says," she smiles. Predictable. She watches the tension slip off our backs. Aromatherapy free with every sale. Along the shelves are cast-iron pots, rough looking, but lift the lid and look, shiny enamel inside, black and smooth. Save your money; they're not cheap, but oh how lovely to see, to touch, to brew in.

Now the counter, worn wooden surface, reassuringly old and functional. The tea crates stacked in the corner, and shelves, long shelves, with tea tins all bearing clear labels: Dragon's Well, Temple of Heaven, Silver Pearl, Eyebrow, Sacred Mountain, Gunpowder, Cloud and Mist, Hairpoint, Jingting Green Snow, Wild Tree, Kooloo, Lingyun White Down, Melon Seeds, Green Snail Spring, Floating World, Qiangang Brilliant White, Green

Summit, Smoked Xinjiang, Tunxi Green, White Down Silver
Needles, Silverpoint, Fire Green, Jade Dew, Purple Bamboo,
Formosa Jade, Sencha, Hojicha, Matcha, Kukicha—the greens.
Darjeeling, Assam, Ceylon, Black Dragon, Keemun, Lapsan
Souchong, English Breakfast, Irish Breakfast, Scottish Breakfast,
Russian—the blacks. Butterfly of Taiwan, Formosa Choice, Dung
Ti, Bao Zhong, Asian Beauty—the Oolongs. Moving farther along,
the flavored teas: Earl Grey, Apricot, Monk's Blend, Blood
Orange, Black Currant, Chai, Strawberry, Blueberry, Raspberry,
Blackberry, Huckleberry, Lemon Grass, Mountain Flower,
Sunflower, Rose, Vanilla, Mango, Pineapple, Chocolate Mint,
Eight Treasures of Shaolin, Mandarin, Peach, Wild Cherry, 1,001
Nights, Christmas Spice, Almond, Hazelnut Cream. And finally
the herbal teas: Rooibos, Honeybush, Yerba Mate, Jasmine,
Spearmint, Ginseng, Peppermint, Chamomile, Cranberry,
Echinacea, Hibiscus.

Can the nose take any more? Scoop in hand, the owner lifts a
sample for us to smell. "Never get that in a bagged tea," she says.

Difficult to describe the smell of a great big scoop of tea, like
rain on dry earth, like petals shaken from the wind, like a forest at
the break of dawn, a meadow at the end of August, a field of hay
in autumn. Feather light and aromatic, essential oils erupt from
the dried leaves. This is tea, this moment of inhaling, wanting to
go on inhaling forever, to bring those smells into every cell, to
bathe our nerves in the presence of those colors, making ourselves green as jasmine or golden as oolong.

Tea and Zen

> "Tea tempers the spirit and harmonizes the mind, dispels lassitude and relieves fatigue; awakens thought and prevents drowsiness . . . Its liquor is like the sweetest dew of heaven."
>
> —Lu Yu, *Cha Ching*

Lu Yu, the grandfather of tea, wrote those words in 780 C.E. An original book, *Cha Ching* (or *Tea Classic*) summed up everything that was known about tea up to that point, including the picking, drying, and preparation of the leaves that were used to create the beverage we know today as green tea. Black tea did not exist, and would not exist for another 864 years. Nevertheless, *Tea Classic* was an exhaustive guide and gave tea drinking high-class appeal.

Tea drinking had been going on in China since 2737 B.C.E. when a wise emperor named Shen Nung first discovered the value of the leaf as a medicine. Over the years the drinking of tea developed into an art with prescribed rules of preparation and etiquette, and by the time Lu Yu wrote his book, China was the largest empire on Earth and traded tea with everyone who was anyone.

What follows is the story of tea, abridged and brief, but enough of the story so that you will be able to understand something important about tea. First of all, that it is old, not just as a plant, but old in the bones of culture, sabi old, worn and reworked, and fashioned and lost and found. Second that it is wabi, the original "wabi," born in the fire of a political forge.

Before tea, *wabi* meant poor. After tea, *wabi* came to mean a spiritual ideal that echoed peace against the walls of war. Wabi is at the center of tea and this chapter is at the center of this book. This story is about "the way of tea," an outgrowth of Zen Buddhism, which was an outgrowth of Buddhism, which was an outgrowth of earlier religious and spiritual teachings. Tea is always a basic beverage, but the way of tea grows, evolves. The tea ceremony in Japan is static, a ritualized form that perfectly relays the values of an age. The way of tea moves on, winding its way through time under the banner of a simple leaf, reminding and rewinding the code of social grace. Tea is and always has been an occasion for friendship, and as the story unfolds you will see that around the bowl of tea, people sit. They talk and share downtime, they teach and meditate together, and they bow and serve each other. Tea is a way of life.

Tea's beginnings in Japan

Early in the ninth century, Kukai, patriarch of the Shingon sect of Buddhism, brought tea, in the form of compressed bricks, from China to the Japanese court. While the tea was met with mild indifference, Buddhism was not. Mount Hiei Monastery stressed enlightenment through religious education and was destined to become a major center for Tendai Buddhism. Many of the monks who graduated from the monastery went on to hold positions in court and in the government, so that over time the monastery grew to be the most influential institution in the country. At the monastery, they drank imported Chinese tea.

In Japan, tea became associated with Buddhism. That association flavored tea for a long time with the scent of religion. It was the Buddhist monks and priests who knew how to prepare and serve tea, and with that knowledge an unseen power became embedded in the preparation and drinking of it. That unseen power was ritual.

A ceremony involving tea was an integral part of Zen, and as Zen spread, so did tea. A monk named Eisai planted tea seeds in Kyoto, near the castle of Fukuoka in the temple grounds of Shokokuji. The plants that grew produced excellent crops because the climate was conducive to growing tea. Up until this time, tea in Japan was largely a drink of the monks, but Eisai was enthusiastic about the medicinal benefits of tea and published his knowledge on the subject in 1214 in a book called *The Book of Tea Sanitation*. When the samurai warrior Sanemoto fell ill after a long night of drinking alcohol, Eisai served him tea. The tea revived Sanemoto, and he therefore promoted it within his circle of samurai family and friends.

The samurai were powerful and well-educated military men. They appreciated Zen's emphasis on discipline and austerity, and they took a liking to tea and learned of the Chinese tradition of using tea drinking as an opportunity to discuss politics and current affairs. They also appreciated its stimulant effect for long watches and sieges. When not actively engaged in warfare, many samurai were farmers who sought balance in accordance with Taoist philosophy and other religious systems in line with the idea of yin and yang. The ceremonies associated with tea at that time had the feel of a spiritual discipline. Tea could be practiced and perfected and it provided a peaceful balance to a samurai's life of conflict and war.

Dogen

Dogen Kigen (1200–1253) studied at the Tendai Monastery on Mount Hiei and under Eisai at the Kenninji Temple, but went on to Zen monasteries in China. These monasteries taught that the practice of Buddhism did not have a formula for enlightenment. There were not two stages of the Zen experience, first practice, then enlightenment. Instead, practice and realization were one. Dogen had intuitively known this all along. Dogen founded the Soto sect of Zen Buddhism in Japan.

If Rinzai, the kind of Zen in which koans brings enlightenment, was known as the school of the samurai, Soto became known as the school of the farmer, a school that stressed not a dramatic awakening, but a gradual acknowledgment of awakening through meditation. Like a tea seed that contains the code necessary for a mature tea tree, humans contain enlightenment at birth. Enlightenment, like the fully mature tea tree, is always in the process of becoming, requiring only time and cultivation to develop.

Dogen was also an enthusiastic tea drinker. He and his students valued tea's stimulant effect for their long hours of meditation. In 1227 Dogen returned from China with a wide assortment of tea utensils and firsthand knowledge about how to use them. In his instructions on daily life at the Eiheiji Temple, he gave detailed instructions for tea ceremonies based on what he had learned in China.

From monastery to castle

In the fifteenth and sixteenth centuries, a newly prosperous and influential merchant class developed in Japan and tea became available to a wider circle of people. Less-formal types of tea drinking developed as they had in China. *Tocha,* a guessing game in which tea tasters attempted to distinguish between the more than 100 varieties of tea grown in Japan at the time, became a popular game at social gatherings. The popularization of tea drinking contributed to the rise of tea stalls where people could buy a bowl of whipped tea from a vendor for a very modest sum. It was during this period that the uneasy dichotomy between tea as a spiritual experience and tea as an opportunity for collecting and displaying tea-related objects began to take shape.

The Shoguns and various wealthy nobles loved the Chinese pots, bowls, and other utensils used in the making of tea. Collecting these items became a fashionable part of their military and business exploits. But a growing number of people who drank tea as a part of their religious life were uncomfortable with tea's new role in the collecting sprees of the elite. Ikkyu (1394–1481), a prince who became a priest, successfully guided some nobles away from what he saw as the corruption of the tea ceremony.

Shuko

Murata Shuko (1422–1503) was a tea master and pupil of Ikkyu who saw that tea could be more than an opportunity for a glitzy party as the nobles saw it, more than a religious ceremony as the monks and priests saw it, and more than a tasteful drink and medicine as the merchants saw it.

Shuko, like all tea masters of his time, was a Zen priest and realized that the preparation and drinking of tea was a deep expression of Zen belief itself. It affirmed and magnified the idea that every act of daily life could lead to enlightenment. Fortunately for Shuko, Shogun Yoshimasa encouraged painting, drama, and tea, and invited Shuko to create a tea ceremony just for him, a sort of commissioned work of art.

Shuko used his new position to take the tea ceremony in a more spiritual direction. The samurai liked to drink tea on a second-story balcony from which they could view the full moon. Referring to this habit, Shuko said, "I have no taste for the full moon." The full moon is perfect and spectacular, but Shuko preferred the half-moon, which, while less bright, is more interesting because of the shadows created by the angle of the sunlight on its surface. While less perfect and less spectacular, the half-moon or the moon partially hidden by clouds also has a more subtle beauty.

Shuko saw the lustrous Chinese bowls and utensils as full moons, and he sought out Japanese artists who could craft items less ostentatious and more subtle. In imitation of rural fishing huts and farming buildings, he designed a small and separate teahouse, because the smaller space produced a more intimate and meaningful experience. Shuko said that the essence of tea and Zen were the same, to help a person participate fully in the art of life. Shuko wove art into the ceremony so that participants experienced the reality of simple courtesy, the potency of patient and direct sensory perception, and the subtlety of natural beauty. His wabi tea was designed to calm a participant's mind and harmonize his whole being with nature.

Jo-o

Takeno Jo-o (1502–1555) studied tea from two of Shuko's disciples and poetry from a noble named Sanetaka. Sanetaka was a classical artist who taught Shuko the art of composing thirty-one–syllable Japanese odes. Jo-o learned his lessons well and because of his strong intuition and natural ability to put things together, he used his poetic talent to express the ideas that Shuko's disciples had instilled in him.

By putting the tea ceremony to verse, Jo-o moved the art of life that Shuko had envisioned to a deeper level. As a tea master Jo-o simplified the small tearoom preferred by Shuko and replaced the white-papered walls with unadorned earthen ones. He used latticework of bamboo instead of finely finished wood and framed the room itself with wood that still retained its coat of bark. Though he himself was wealthy, he held his wealth at a distance from the sacred space of the tearoom and preferred a simple setting of plain utensils. Jo-o was that wise instructor who set the eager young Rikyu to work in his garden to test his intuition of wabi sabi.

Rikyu

Sen no Rikyu (1522–1591) became the chief tea master for Hideyoshi. He stripped everything nonessential from the tearoom and the method of preparation, and developed a tea ritual in which there was no wasted movement and no object that was superfluous. This emphasis on the exact movement of hands and utensils was partly to guard against breakage and partly to emphasize the grace that can be achieved in daily activities like the preparation of tea.

Rikyu further stabilized the tea ceremony and ensured that it met Hideyoshi's criteria for a ceremony that could reconcile the differences between the warring provinces he had united. He found a way to foster peace of mind, which allowed participants to see and face the disharmony in the rest of their lives.

The ceremony itself

Rikyu described the ceremony this way: "Make a delicious bowl of tea; lay the charcoal so that it heats the water; arrange the flowers as they are in the field; in summer suggest coolness; in winter, warmth; do everything ahead of time; prepare for rain; and give those with whom you find yourself every consideration." The ceremony is a sort of scripted drama in which everyone knows their part and finds pleasure in immersing themselves in the role.

Rikyu felt that the aim of Zen was to purify the soul by becoming one with nature; so he used only obviously natural elements in his tearoom, such as bamboo, reed, clay, and wood. He situated the tearoom in a garden, away from other buildings, to create a sacred space, centered in nature. Natural elements were appreciated by educated and uneducated alike, and simple elements suggested the common nature that all humans share, regardless of class or position in life.

Participants entered the garden by a gate, symbolically leaving the cares of the world outside. The sense of entering a liminal world was further reinforced as the participant proceeded across stepping-stones or along a winding path. The path itself was usually sprinkled with water ahead of time to bring to mind purity and the cleansing nature of rain and dew.

The tea hut was prefaced with a covered porch in which participants removed their shoes and donned white *tabi,* a kind of Japanese sock. Rikyu placed a washbasin nearby in which participants could wash their hands and mouths, further reinforcing the role of purity in action and speech.

Leaving the dust of the world behind, cleansed and wearing new and pure footwear, participants next removed their swords, leaving them, with their shoes, outside. Rikyu designed his tea huts with a low, small door that could not be entered upright or wearing a sword. Samurai and other powerful leaders found this act of crawling into the tea hut to be psychologically disarming. Once inside the small inner chamber, participants immediately saw a simple display of chosen art such as a scroll, painting, or piece of ceramic. Along with this single art object was a simple flower arrangement. It was understood that the participants would spend some time noticing these objects since they were the only ornaments in the room. Polite conversation at this point would revolve around the art objects and tea utensils.

At that point, Rikyu would serve a light meal or *kaiseki* (bosom stone). This term came from the habit of monks who, in attempts to overcome hunger, would place warmed stones on their stomachs. *Kaiseki* was not intended to satiate hunger completely, but to remind participants of the role of food in their lives and the simple pleasure of eating. During this light meal, Rikyu would clean and prepare the bowls and utensils. This was the part of the ceremony that required the greatest choreography and training for tea masters. Like a dance of the hands, the movements of washing and drying and making the tea all were done with grace, balance, and care.

The burning of the charcoal, the boiling of the water, and the sound of bamboo on the earthenware bowls became amplified in the small and intimate space. Participants could ponder the elemental balance at work in the utensils. All the primary elements of the Taoist system were present (metal, wood, water, fire, and earth), and their interaction brought completeness to the ritual. After the tea had been made in the traditional manner with powdered tea and whisk, further ritualized courtesy was prescribed. The first guest would receive the bowl with a bow and say, "Excuse me for drinking before you," and "I gratefully accept the tea you have prepared." After drinking the three and a half mouthfuls in the cup, the guest would wipe and examine the bowl, commenting on its unique nature and beauty. Rikyu gave tea-bowl designs to a tile maker named Chojiro. Chojiro was later given the name *Raku,* and the Raku family tradition of pottery has continued to flourish for more than 400 years. Raku embodies wabi by producing imperfect shapes that are interesting to hold and pleasant to the lips. They use crackle glaze and natural colorations and patterns to reinforce the feeling of sabi beauty. The tea caddy and other utensils were then appreciated. Each guest in turn would receive the same treatment in unhurried tranquility. The ceremony might last for up to four hours.

The ritual in action

In the grandest gesture of his political career, Rikyu's patron, Hideyoshi, attempted to stretch the tea ceremony wide enough to embrace all classes of Japanese culture. At a famous gathering of tea celebrants initiated by Hideyoshi, the two contrasting styles of tea drinking were brought into clear view. There were those who preferred the rich and ostentatious Shoin style of celebration, and those who preferred the lowly wabi celebrations, begun by Shuko, continued by Jo-o, and formalized by Rikyu. The wabi tea ceremony brought guests together and gently stripped them of rank or status. It transformed participants into members of a larger value system, unifying them in a culture of peace. Because this was valued both by the powerful Shogun and by the common person, it became a national ritual.

Your wabi sabi friends

As beautiful as the tea ceremony was, and still is, it exists for most of us as a lovely but elaborate ritual, impractical in our busy lives but luminously present in our imaginations. And perhaps this is an appropriate place for it, because as inspiration it can guide real and practical efforts to manifest all that it represents in our life today.

Start by exploring tea itself. Take a friend to a teashop with you. Ask questions, make careful purchases, and learn to savor the flavors of each kind of tea. Consider participating in the tea ceremony itself. In most large urban areas, there are both Chinese and Japanese tea masters who will be happy to introduce you to their unique art. Chinese tea ceremonies focus on the taste and smell of the tea, providing a truly sensual experience. Japanese tea ceremonies are careful re-creations of Rikyu's own ceremonies and impart peace and tranquility along with the tea. These novel experiences can enrich your friendships. Introduce your friends to the world of tea and honor the spiritual impact it can have on your friendships. Become an Eisai and explore the health benefits of tea. Model your entertaining on Shuko and Rikyu, share intimate and unhurried meals with friends in simple surroundings. Forget the fancy restaurants. A poignant memory for me is sipping tea from a thermos cup after a day of fishing with my father. Tea lends itself to outdoors, to campfires and cross-country skiing. It can be prepared with minimal equipment.

Three of Rikyu's principal students were devout Christians: Furuta Oribe, Takayama Ukon, and Gamou Ujisato. The way of tea can enrich any tradition; the Zen ideal of nonattachment can deepen the life of any open-minded believer. Nonattachment is not the same as detachment. The tea ceremony demonstrates that when we focus on creating a peaceful and courteous space for others, we lose ourselves in the process. When we cut the strings of attachment to our friends we allow them to exist apart from our control. This does not mean being impersonal, impolite, or aloof. Nonattachment just means removing the need to force others to be like us, acknowledging that our friends can see things differently from us, and enjoying the differences as added texture in our relationships. It observes with knowing fondness the individual traits that make each person her own self, hobbling, or striding, or careening along a path all her own. It means accepting that the differences in people's lives are icing on the fundamental human cake. People's hearts are much the same, while their unique patterns of living unfold like fiddlehead ferns from the ground of being. In the same way that Rikyu crafted an environment that de-emphasized class and status, your own circle of influence can welcome people who are different than you, making a place for them in the grand canvas of your inner imagination.

The tea ceremony encoded values in a ritualized form. Hygiene was stressed in the washing of face and bowls; economics was demonstrated with unhurried comfort in a simple space, and taste and style were implied by proportion and context. What do your own rituals say about you? What practices do you engage in that reinforce your values, that artfully encapsulate your own ideas and priorities? What things do you wish you could be better at? Can you ritualize behaviors you want so that they mold you into the better person you know you can be? Is your personal space a reflection of who you really are? Can you strip away things from life that keep you from direct experience of the moment, that keep you wrapped in memory, or looking to some future goal? Memories are inevitable and goals are practical, but simple existence is always with you.

No one needs too much of anything. Remember the proverb affirmed by Tokugawa Ieyasu, "Enough is as good as a feast." When you invite friends to share a meal with you, don't feel you have to wow them with luxury. The world is full of people trying to out-do and out-impress others. Let that world go and embrace the way of tea. People will always respond to harmony, respect, tranquility, and purity. Let those qualities guide you. The art of life is turning yourself toward people, not toward outcomes.

A person of tea, wabi tea, sees that power struggles and politics must not outweigh forthright honesty and peace. The violent tendencies of humans can be addressed with gentle arts. Wabi art creates simple unpretentious beauty and in so doing allows all who wish to enter. Opulent beauty can be intimidating, overlain with expectation, underwritten with hidden agendas, and concealed motives. Wabi beauty invites humility, the negation of self-centered absorption. In the presence of a wabi soul, people come to rest. They drop their guard and breathe a sigh of relief. In Rikyu's time, Muichibutsu were wabi people who did not possess tea bowls and pots, and they did not long to have them, not even the simplest utensil. They were free of attachments and passion for possession. If they had no tea, they drank water; if they had tea but nothing to boil it in, they gave the tea to someone who did, or they asked to borrow what was needed and shared what they had.

There is a new batch of tea leaves every year, but tea, the archetypal tea, is old, sabi old. Those who make a choice to become nonattached make their life sabi. And if they do this without drawing attention to the change, they make themselves wabi. The wabi sabi way is one in which the passage of time is noted, accepted, and released. Tea does not keep in a jar forever; it continues to break down over time and becomes tasteless. So does a life kept in a jar. When you serve and enjoy tea, you acknowledge its transitory nature, allowing it to represent all things, sipping away at impermanence itself. All you really need to do is make a delicious bowl of tea, arrange flowers, and think about your friends and give them your every consideration. Simple to imagine, the proof is in the tea.

How to be a wabi sabi listener

For a tea master the tea ceremony is an exercise in paying constant attention to his or her guests. The choreographed actions, practiced over and over again, ensure that attention to the guest barely needs to waver in the preparation of tea. The body performs the menial tasks out of habit so that attention can be given to the joy of meeting.

Imagine a friend named Mary comes to you with a problem. Mary will have a hard time hearing anything you say until she has had a chance to be heard, had a chance to speak her mind. If you can listen and not comment, eventually she might solve the problem herself. Zen teachers often stress that everyone is sufficient in himself or herself. It is always a joy to see this occur in another person's life. The reason it happens is that when Mary's thoughts and feelings are rolling around inside her head, they are too close, as if a message was written on the surface of her eyeglasses. By talking about these exact feelings and thoughts and tagging them with real language, animating them in a story, or a sequence, uttering what is inside and making it public, this act itself can break the size illusion that things up close can have. Speaking into the air so that she can hear herself saying them, she gains an amazing perspective. Mary hears herself talking about things that take on new light in the presence of a human other, a respectful listener. A good listener is a mirror, a sounding board, and a tennis partner who reflects/echoes/returns the thoughts and emotions so that they can be heard, seen, and felt with some objectivity. A good listener is the paper on which the message is placed so that the speaker can finally see what was folded too tightly inside to read.

Carl Rogers is considered one of the all-time best listeners. Much of his success as a therapist came from his ability to listen wholeheartedly to his patients. Rogers practiced being genuinely honest, empathetic, and respectful. To listen in this way requires a conscious decision to suspend your own needs and thoughts while you focus on the other person. Just like the tea master allowing his body to do the beautiful motions involved in making the tea while his regard is on his guest, a good listener allows her body to offer the necessary social cues while her attention focuses on the person in every detail.

Too often we make the mistake of listening only to the words a person is saying. Or we allow our minds to wander off with threads of the conversation and play with them, failing to respect the growing tapestry that the person is making. Children are particularly good at picking up on body language and other nonverbal cues, but over time the force of words and language clouds this ability. With a little self-discipline you can learn to renotice other areas of behavior that accompany talking, and once you have again become aware of them you can let them inform your listening. And most remarkable of all, once you notice what a person is really saying both verbally and with his or her body language, you will also begin to notice other communications going on around you, the context of the relationship speaking its own language. Suddenly you will see that there is an irrational and subtle connection to the world of nature and people that is much more interesting than the connections you consciously try to make yourself.

The strings of the metaworld that vibrate the core of all creation respond to human expression like the strings of an instrument respond when you sing close to them. A bird will punctuate an idea with its song, a passing train will illustrate the journey of the mind, or a sudden rainstorm will drench you symbolically like the rain of peace you desire. It will be as if the universe listens, too, mirroring back the salient points, demonstrating in spontaneous reflections the topic of conversation. By immersing yourself into this third-level listening, your own desires and fears and motivations will be bathed in the real and expanding world of the other, the Christ in everyone, the light in us all. Such beauty is beyond possession. This is the way of tea.

Six
Wabi sabi at work

in line at the bank

little girl jumps with both feet

over a bug

摸

WHEN I WAS A STUDENT I worked for several summers at a telephone company. In those days all long-distance telephone calls were connected by an automated system that included rows and rows of magnetic switches and stacked pancakes of circuit boards along which a mechanical arm would travel and swing in at the right spot to make the connection. As part of my job, for several weeks every summer I would climb up a ladder and, armed with a can of Freon gas and various mildly abrasive pads, would proceed to clean each connection—thousands of them, for hours on end. Time has never gone so slowly in all my life. I remember working steadily, cleaning, willing myself not to look at my watch, and finally giving in and seeing that only five minutes had gone by since the last time I looked.

I now use that experience as an important marker on what I call my "flow scale." That experience is on the very end of the scale labeled "no flow." At the other end is the experience I have when I lose myself in writing, or creating graphic designs, or working in the garden. At this pleasant end of the scale I am "in flow," the magical state of being, in which time becomes a mere abstraction and in which the now, the moment, opens with meaning and fulfillment. Different people achieve flow differently, but according to psychologist and author Mihaly Csikszentmihalyi, there are several factors that contribute to a state of flow. The first is clarity of goals and rules. When you know what is required and how to get there, you can really focus on the task. Second, you need immediate feedback as you go along to tell you how you are doing. Direct sensory feedback is best, so that you hear, see, and feel the effects of your actions. I think this is why artists enter flow easily; they immediately see the effect of their actions in the medium in which they are working. Third, your personal skills should engage in overcoming a manageable challenge, one that you feel you can handle without too much stress. If the job is too demanding and you don't think you can do it, fear and anxiety will prevent flow. If the job is not demanding enough, or if you see it as below your skill level, boredom will also get in the way of flow. And, finally, give a task the right amount of time. Flow often occurs twenty to thirty minutes into an activity. There is a wabi sabi way to increase flow when you work, but before we can discuss that subject, one of the psychological mechanisms behind work needs to be brought to light.

Why you fight for what you want and the wabi sabi alternative

Let me introduce you to Kim, a two-year-old playing in the toddler room, toys spread all over the floor around her. Now meet Kevin, a fellow two-year-old who has just entered the room where Kim is. See him scanning all the toys? He smiles, makes a happy sound, then he sees Kim, playing intently with a blue jack-in-the-box. It springs open. Kevin toddles toward her, chubby legs brushing each other, arms outstretched toward the jack-in-the-box. He grabs it and starts to pull, using his diapered posterior for ballast. Kim makes a loud noise and says firmly, "No." Kevin pulls harder and gets the box away from her. She starts to cry. The caregiver comes and soothes Kim, gets her interested in another toy, and when she is happy, leaves again.

Kevin sees Kim playing with a new toy, a stuffed alligator named Ruthy Toothy. Kevin abandons the jack-in-the-box and wrestles Ruthy out of Kim's arms. Kim, tired of this treatment, pushes Kevin over and takes Ruthy back. She starts to run away but Kevin is faster; he pushes her from behind and she falls, lucky for Kim, into a pile of foam blocks. The caregiver sees this, seizes Kevin by the arm, and takes him to the corner to talk to him. "You have to be nice to Kim. No pushing allowed." With his big eyes wide open, he looks at the caregiver and says, "Kim pushed me first." He is as honest as Ruthy's teeth.

Kevin, whether he knows it or not, has started work. For the rest of his life, he will be doing what he can to get what he wants. And much of what he wants will be things other people have. He will want them because others have them, and when he has them, he will enjoy them only briefly, and then start looking for something new. What is this strange human tendency to want what others have? Kevin could have chosen Ruthy Toothy when he first came into the room. But he didn't even notice her. Instead, he went for the toy in Kim's hands. This deep-rooted tendency to want what others have and to go about getting it is called "mimesis" and is the motivating factor for much of the work we do.

Over the last few years scholars have worked to identify and understand the various ways that this human tendency manifests itself in culture. It partially explains why the "popular" girl is so popular when girls who are just as nice and just as pretty go unnoticed. It is why celebrities rise like meteors and then fall quickly from favor. It is a significant factor in the stock market and phenomena like the popularity of Pogs and Pokemon; in fact, it can be found at the root of most fads. It explains tattooing, fashion, and trendy nightclubs and restaurants. Wherever people gather to do the latest thing, there you will see mimesis.

Mimetic theory suggests that the same pattern that occurred in the playroom between Kim and Kevin occurs between humans of all ages and leads inevitably to scapegoating. Think of your favorite action movie. Regardless of the details, a predictable element will likely be present. There will be a hero who must fight against or outwit an evil enemy. Often the enemy will appear overwhelmingly powerful and will abuse power and show no mercy. In the rest of the story, the hero will go through harrowing experiences to complete a mission and ultimately defeat the evil enemy. Sometimes the characters will be brothers, or father and son, one normal like us, and the other twisted and evil, such as Luke and Anakin Skywalker in *Star Wars* or the Elves and the Orcs in *Lord of the Rings*. Sometimes the evil enemies are machines, as in *The Matrix*, or an alien species, as in the *Alien* movies or *Men in Black*.

Sorting people into good guys and bad guys is part of the mimetic mechanism. Once we know who the good guy is, we can imitate his behavior. If the bad guy uses violence, in our eyes he is even more threatening as an enemy, so we root for the good guy and delight when he reveals his secret weapon, which undoes the evil villain. We happily overlook the violent behavior of the good guy, the hero, because he is in the right, on our side, and usually good-looking.

Propagandists know the power of mimesis and exploit it to their advantage. A country at war often describes its opponent as an expendable other, a less than human "them." *They* are described as being selfish, ignorant, threatening, or greedy. In order for "civilized people" to be violent toward others, we must justify our actions. It can't be that we just want to take what others have, or keep them from having what we have. Like Kevin, most people learn early on to camouflage this basic desire. So we tell ourselves that we deserve what we have and they don't. We are more civilized, more responsible, more democratic, more cultured, smarter, wiser, stronger, braver. We have better genes, better brains, better customs, and better traditions. If only we can eliminate "them," our lives will be better, peace will return, and we can get on with enjoying all our stuff. Once a person or a group of people is seen as the scapegoat, by killing, expelling, or defeating them, we expect to eliminate conflict. In the scapegoat system, there is no solution for conflict, only a temporary way of dealing with it.

Some people are tempted to think that if everyone had enough, there would be no reason for conflict. But status is a part of mimesis. It is based on the idea that only a select few can own this item, only the chosen can be taught this secret knowledge, only those passing a difficult series of tests can enter this fraternity or profession. Only those dressing a certain way can enter this club, only those with the right stuff can play on this team, enter this training school, or park in this parking spot. When status is at stake, mimesis ensures that people will compete to be admitted, often for no better reason than inclusion itself.

You will see this form of the mimetic mechanism at work in teams, companies, religions, and groups of all kinds. Once a person is included in the group, he or she becomes a part of "we" and "us" and takes on the group's desire to win. The collective "they" or "them" become opponents, or even "the enemy." In war, sports, religion, commerce, and school, competition produces allies and enemies.

Athletes prove that competition pushes people to levels of performance they might not otherwise achieve. The desire to win is a strong motivator. Companies demonstrate that competition spurs on workers. Higher productivity, more efficient methods of production, and more innovative designs ensure more sales and more stuff for everyone to do and buy. Competition is a deep-seated value, supported by mimesis and embraced by many people who want to win, beat the other guy, or simply prove their superiority.

Wabi sabi challenges the assumption that competition is good. It asks: Is competition the only motivator to excellence? Does competition encourage the values we would rationally choose to foster in our children and ourselves? Does competition produce excellent peace? Does it produce excellent tranquility? Excellent mutual respect, cooperation, and self-confidence? Does it produce excellent contentment? An excellent environment or excellent working conditions? Does competition produce excellent compassion? Excellent wisdom? Excellent loving kindness?

Just where is it that competition shines? Sports and commerce seem to rely on it, and when we apply for a new job we compete with other applicants.

A question that needs to be asked in the face of an aggressively competitive world is, how do the losers feel? Do their feelings contribute to a better society? Do losers make good parents, spouses, and workers? Do losers learn more, contribute more, and produce more? Wabi sabi points to the reality that in a competitive world there are far more losers than there are winners.

Many people value competitive sports and a competitive work environment because the goals are clear, the rules are defined, and flow is experienced. If you can face the challenge, if you are confident in your abilities, each new game or contract is an opportunity to lose yourself in flow. If you are not confident in your abilities or if you feel the challenge is too great or, conversely, too small, work will be hard and long. If you are in that situation now, the easiest way to bring wabi sabi to your work might be to bring yourself to work that is more suited to you, your personality, and your abilities.

Competition and mimesis are always with us, but if you can see these things for what they are and face your challenges honestly, you will become authentic in your work. If you thrive on competition and find flow in the games of life, remember that competition has drawbacks. It produces dichotomy, delineation, distinction, and is essentially divisive. Enjoy the flow but remember that others find flow in different ways. Making competition a bedrock virtue, enshrined in the tomes of success, only ensures more stress in the culture of excess.

Wabi sabi does not criticize winners. In its steady and under-stated way it points out that all winnings and the factors that lead to a win are impermanent. They do not last. Winners do not stay winners; someone stronger, faster, smarter, or meaner will come along. If you have something, it will be taken away. Only what you give to others is truly yours, because you give it to someone before it is taken from you by force, age, circumstance, or chance.

Taking the wabi sabi view of life does not mean you throw up your hands and do nothing, letting events come in and out of your life in a placid stream from birth to death. Instead, it means that you maintain an overriding conscious perspective that no job is per-fect, no job is forever, and no job finishes completely. If a position on the team, or a promotion, or a sign of status is given to you, in wabi sabi humility you will appreciate the honor and rejoice in the moment, and if someone else is promoted or recognized instead of you, your wabi sabi wisdom will help you understand that this is the way things work. You can analyze the process and see why you missed out and why the other person got the prize. You can become aware of your desires and discern if you want something because of its own merit or because everyone else is scrambling to get it. Wabi sabi work allows your attention to flow and your unique talents and abilities to grow. Treat status as a by-product of mimesis and do not be deceived by it. If you are smart and tal-ented, remember that these are gifts from your genetic makeup, based on factors over which you had no control. If you are not smart or talented, the same attitude will see you through.

The wabi sabi way is gentle and humble and recognizes compe-tition and status as human tendencies, not human virtues. Instead of focusing on conflict and competition, wabi sabi points to harmony, respect, tranquility, and purity. It affirms the values of reputation, friendship, generosity, contentment, acceptance, wisdom, knowledge, good deeds, kindness, thoughtfulness, and creativity. With these values in mind, you will be better able to judge the authenticity of your various desires and reorient yourself amid the vast array of possessions and positions you see in the world around you.

To counteract the negative effects of mimesis, turn it to your advantage. Pick someone you admire, someone who is her own person, someone who you think is a morally upright and balanced individual, successful because she uses her unique gifts and abilities in an honest and authentic way. It might be someone like Jesus or Buddha or Mother Teresa or Eleanor Roosevelt, or it might be someone like your father or mother or a teacher or a mentor. Hold that person in your mind as a sort of ideal, and when you are tempted to give in to the power of mimesis, ask yourself if that person would give in. When you feel like fighting for something, visualize what your role model would do. When you are tempted to follow the crowd, imagine if that person would follow. Eventually your ideal person will resemble more and more the person you are, and finally it will be you. Imitating great people will make you great, but the final piece in the puzzle of greatness will come to you only when you acknowledge that the ideal person is that individual inside you that is a flavor with your name on it, a pattern of being as unique as your signature, and a creature made alive by your own special magic. The mimetic mechanism is inside you and you can't get rid of it, but with wabi sabi perspective you can use it to become the person you really are.

Avoiding mimetic behaviors

There are wabi sabi ways to avoid being lured into mimetic behaviors:

1. Recognize mimesis as a part of your unconscious motivation. Examine your desires consciously and let go of any that are not valuable.
2. Determine why you want things before you buy or pursue them. Make a list of reasons for and against them. Don't be rushed into commitments or purchases. Wait days or weeks and see if you still desire them.
3. Watch for scapegoating. Is someone being picked on, slandered, stereotyped? This tells you that mimesis is at work. If the people engaged in it are good people in the grip of mimesis, speak up for the victim, dispel the unconscious tendency to vilify and marginalize, and the power of scapegoating will evaporate.
4. If you are fighting with someone, ask yourself if the cause could be mimetic, and if it is, let go of the need to have the last word, let go of the need to be the authority, let go of the need to show someone they are wrong. Let the other person win or look for a way that both of you can win.
5. Point out the mimetic lure of an object, position, or status symbol to those around you. Awareness of it dispels the mimetic influence.
6. Look for wabi sabi qualities in objects. Is it natural, authentic, beautiful, well crafted, proportioned, and not

ostentatious? Does it support your values? Is it available to everyone?

7. Reject fads, trends, and peer pressure. Find your own unique style and stick with it.

8. Enjoy your special talents and abilities and develop a career around them.

9. Pursue excellence for its own sake, not to beat someone else to a prize.

10. Give, expecting nothing in return. Sharing satisfies a deep part of you that hoarding never will. Go beyond the "I owe you one" mentality to the "pay it forward" mentality.

The dangers of owning too many things

Economists have pointed to land ownership as a key factor in the success of the American economy. When you own something, you take responsibility for it. When you have worked hard to purchase something, you take care of it. And when you build a house or business or company, you invest in it. But, however good it may be for the economy as a whole, owning land and possessions has a hidden cost to the individual and a dangerous effect on our perception of reality as a nation.

People in the United States used to save about 8 percent of their income for a rainy day. Now the average is .02 percent. Total household debt in America has soared to more than $5 trillion nationwide. Every few years we "buy up"—a better car, better furniture, a better house, and each time we do we incur more debt. Because lending institutions continue to finance our debt as we move up, we conclude that we are managing and that we are on the right track. The more we have the more we want, until one day we wake up and realize that we are overweight, overstimulated, overindulged, overextended, overcommitted, overdrawn, overanxious, overmedicated, overinsured, and overly concerned about all the things we have. We need to calm down, slow down, slim down, and find balance. But our stuff gets in the way.

Once you have things, you fear losing them. Do you want to go back to renting once you own a house? Do you want to go back to tap water once you are used to bottled or filtered water? Do you want to give up power steering, fleece fabric, and your microwave? So many things that once were luxuries become necessities. The good life becomes the expected lifestyle. Yet in the end you will have to give it all up. We only enjoy things for a season. Nothing lasts, not even you.

One way to recognize this reality is to remind yourself repeatedly of how good the things you have are. The international poverty line is measured by daily income. If a person earns less than $1 or $2 per day, depending on various social and political factors, they are below the line. Are you making more than that $2 a day? If you are, you are one of the lucky few by world standards. In 2003 there were 1.2 billion people living on $1 a day, and another 2.8 billion living on less than $2 a day. By contrast the richest fifth of the world's population received 85 percent of the total world income. If you own a car, a TV set, or a telephone, consider yourself privileged. Only 17.6 percent of the people in the world have a car or other motor vehicle. Only 26.4 percent of people in the world have a television set, and only 17 percent have access to a regular telephone line. It helps to remember this and to ask yourself if you can justify your lifestyle when so many others have so much less.

In the 1920s, corporations in the industrialized world designed a strategy to motivate the public to want more. They did this deliberately to increase sales and therefore profits. They invented a market strategy that created a permanent class of "dissatisfied consumers." Until then, people who earned enough to pay the rent, feed the children, and make contributions to church and society were content, and they didn't feel compelled to keep buying more and more stuff. The past generations' dreams had come true, and to expect more was seen as gluttony and greed. This was partly because, before the 1920s, only the richest members of society realized such stability. This contentment with the basics of life was, of course, a problem for marketers.

Since that time marketers have learned the effectiveness of the mimetic model, placing their products into the hands and on the bodies of the cultural icons. Advertisers apply the status appeal of "cool" to name brands with clever forethought. These efforts have paid off. The average American today consumes twice as much as the average American did fifty years ago. The increase in spending represents an increase in overall income, but this increase in wealth and possessions has not brought a corresponding increase in happiness. Sixty percent of successful professionals surveyed in 1997 reported that they suffered chronic stress and depression. Forty-eight percent of top corporate executives described their lives as empty and meaningless. In the last few years, overworked men and women have begun to wonder if the pursuit of happiness might not involve more than the pursuit of material possessions.

Single-tasking and the quest for simple elegant code

Multitasking, the ability to do more than one thing at a time, has always interested me, largely because I have never really mastered it. Oh, there are times when I will start the photocopier going and return to my desk to finish a letter I am working on, but anything much more complicated than that taxes my capacity. For years I felt bad about this, felt inadequate because I was unable to hold multiple threads of activity in the proper order in my mind at the same time.

Then, a few years ago I heard about single-tasking from computer geeks who expressed their desire to work intensely on one problem before moving on to the next. When a computer is multitasking, it divides its computing power up between programs and gives the illusion that it is doing two things at once. What it is really doing is a bit of one task and a bit of another, alternating, until both tasks are done. Because in human terms it takes little time to execute both tasks, we perceive that the computer accomplishes both simultaneously. The technique obviously doesn't work all the time, because most of us have had that frustrating experience when our computer locks up because too many programs are running at the same time.

About seven years ago I started designing Web pages. At first I dabbled with drag-and-drop software, but that led to an interest in HTML and a short course on advanced HTML techniques. I looked at the code that the drag-and-drop programs created and was not happy with the clutter and redundancy I saw. "Simple elegant code," as it's called in online forums and bulletin boards, produces clean fast-loading pages. I discovered that Web page designers often examine the code of pages they visit, and I too began peeking at the code on other people's pages. When I found "simple elegant code" I would often whisper to myself, "very nice." I was amazed to find a wabi sabi beauty in the world of tech slick.

Multitaskers find flow in the complex weave of multiple threads that make up the fabric of their multiple projects. The challenge for them is to shuttle each thread into the loom at the right time and then shuttle it back out again. Single-taskers plunge into the deep water of a solitary task and swim all the way to the bottom. Like pearl divers, they return triumphantly to the surface of a job with oysters in hand and proceed to crack them open until they find treasure. Are you a multi- or single-tasker? How about the people you work with? Does doing one large task alone bore a multitasker, or do many small tasks overwhelm a single-tasker? By working to match people with their preferences, businesses can become more productive and at the same time allow employees to find a greater level of authentic work.

Multitasking has been in vogue for many years, but immersing in a single job, crafting and reworking it to achieve a simple and elegant result over time, often has more wabi sabi beauty. A tool or design produced in this way does its job simply and effectively year after year, until it becomes a humble resident of the general background of culture and tradition.

Perfected technology and the nature of true craftsmanship

A few winters ago I opened a long rectangular Christmas present and lifted out a tall wooden pepper mill made from a solid piece of maple. Every time I use that mill I enjoy the rich color of the wood, the smooth feel in my hand, and the satisfying crunch and crack of the peppercorns being broken. I love the smell of the fresh pepper rising in the steam from hot food. These moments are rich in wabi sabi feelings. A plastic shaker full of preground pepper just does not provide the same experience.

We humans have been adding to our knowledge for some 5,000 years. The basic routines of daily life over that time have revolved around planting, harvesting, and making the items we need to survive. Many tools and household objects have been crafted and recrafted over the years until they handily match the tasks they serve.

Because we use them over and over and because we also hand some of them down from generation to generation, we grow exceedingly fond of them. For instance, have you noticed how people become attached to their pens? In shared office space, individuals will jealously guard their special pens because pen

thieves abound. Some people collect pens, and these serious collectors tend to go for fountain pens. Fountain pens provide a rich
sensory experience. There is the raspy scratch of the nib on the
paper, the skill required to avoid smearing the ink, and the lovely
lumpy letters that spill along the page in organic shapes accentu-
ated by the ready flow of ink that a fountain pen provides.

I like pencils for their simplicity and reliability.

For those of us who revel in the triumph of elegant simplicity,
civil engineer Henry Petroski's 434-page book about the pencil,
The Pencil: A History of Design and Circumstance, is a satisfying
recounting of the development of an instrument that is imbedded
in our psyche as a tool of imagination and design itself.

Part of what I like about the pencil is its paradoxical nature.
Graphite, the central core of the device, is nicely wabi sabi.
Depending on its formulation it can resist smudging and last on
surfaces much longer than ink ever would. As a teenager I visited
the remains of miner's camps in the mountains around my childhood home and saw penciled notes on old cabin walls and on the
rocks inside the mouths of abandoned mines that remained leg-
ible even after years of exposure to weather and sun. Yet for all its
permanence, the pencil mark can be erased, leaving sometimes a
faint shadow, and sometimes only an impression in the paper.
Hard graphite produces a soft line on the page, does not blob or
run, and resists water damage and fading. So much pleases me
about it, and every time I use my pencil I enjoy its pragmatic
appeal and its contradictory charm.

Simple elegance has always been the goal of a certain class of
designers and engineers. This wabi sabi sensibility has led to the

development of many items we use on a daily basis that are simple and pleasing to the eye. Consider, for example, the potato peeler, ingenious and functional and basically unchanged for more than 100 years. Consider the needle and thread, which have existed since prehistoric times and serve essentially the same function today as they did then. Consider spoons, the most basic of eating utensils, made of wood, ceramic, or metal; their pleasing shape makes eating a joy. The list of wabi sabi items is long. There is the compass, the wheel, the book, paper, the printing press, and writing itself. There are the tools of the garden: the shovel, the rake, and the reed and bamboo baskets. There are the tools of construction: the hammer, the chisel, the saw, and the drill. There are the household items: soap, candles, spinning wheels, and brooms. There are the garment standards: shoes, hats, gloves, shirts, and that essential in the closet—blue jeans. All of them become wabi sabi by being with us for so long, by being caressed in labor, cradled in contemplation, and remembered in reminiscence. Every time we use these things we participate in and reinforce their wabi sabi nature. There is great pleasure in using well-crafted and well-engineered tools and even more pleasure in knowing that they have been used in the same way for hundreds and sometimes thousands of years.

Seven
Wabi sabi relaxation

beside the swollen Chase River

smelling and then finding

violets

ON A COLD DECEMBER MORNING a bobcat, furry with stealth, deliberates like a shadowy mist through a grove of ice-encrusted pine trees. After a slow crouch, vibrating, she pounces toward a camouflaged white hare. Instantly the hare leaps away sideways and off through the wintry glade. The bobcat twists after the hare, her large grasping paws connecting briefly with the bounding hare. In this magnified moment both animals experience a powerful flood of hormones into their systems resulting in flight across the snow. The bobcat needs to catch and eat the hare to survive and the hare needs to get away and hide to survive. Both animals have mechanisms that allow them to bring all their bodily resources to this intense moment of competition for life.

Anyone privileged to watch such a display marvels at the speed of the hare, each huge arcing leap in the air, with long hind limbs fully extended behind it, an impressive demonstration of lever action. We may marvel, as well, at the bobcat as she twists and contorts to try to snare the *Lepus americanus*. The snowshoe hare's heart pounds; breath is rapid; fuel and oxygen flood the muscles. Blood pressure goes up, arteries tighten, and pupils widen to take in all the visual information possible. The brain triggers this optimal state for intense physical performance by sending neural signals, a classic example of the fight-or-flight response.

Such dramas conclude quickly if the bobcat catches the hare and kills it. But this day in the deep powdery snow, the light, lucky, agile hare has a margin of advantage and manages to stay one paw-length ahead until the large feline expends her intense but brief spurt of energy. Bounding on its long snowshoe feet, the hare disappears from sight into the forest. When it finally stops, it will find an opening in the snow-well at the bottom of a fir tree and crawl in under the lowest branches where it is dark and safe, and there it will stay for several hours while its heart rate slows, pupils constrict, and breathing slows. Eventually its digestion will resume, and it will start to feel hungry again. It will then venture out to find food, into the dangerous winter land we call wonder.

These two responses, the "fight-or-flight" and the "rest and digest," represent two functionally separate systems within the larger autonomic nervous system. The sympathetic nervous system produces the fight-or-flight response, characterized by an increase in blood pressure and heart rate, a constriction of blood vessels, an opening of the airways, and a slowing of the gut. Other effects include the dilation of the pupils, drying of the mouth, mobilization of stored fat, suppression of the immune system, increase in appetite, and a decrease in sensitivity to pain.

After the crisis is over, the parasympathetic system takes over; it slows the heart, dilates the blood vessels, relaxes the airways, boots up the immune system, reorients the pain receptors, constricts the pupils, and speeds up digestions and the movement of the bowels. This is the part of the autonomic nervous system that tells the body to rest and digest.

After an emergency is over, animals seek out dark quiet places so they can lick their wounds and recover. If they are together with others of their kind, they will lick and groom and soothe each other. These actions directly stimulate the amygdala, an almond-shaped structure at the base of the limbic system that is responsible for both the sympathetic and parasympathetic responses. During an emergency this complex bundle of nerves interprets the scents, sounds, and visual images extremely efficiently. The amygdala's speed of functioning is what allows the hare to react so quickly, and via direct neural messaging and split-second hormonal response, the hare's whole body is brought into a profound state of alertness. In the same way, the darkness and stillness under the fir tree removes stimulation from the amygdala and after a prescribed amount of time the small brain structure prompts the parasympathetic system to calm and restore the body.

Humans have amygdalas similar to those of the hare and the bobcat. Perched above the brainstem and below the limbic ring, the amygdala in humans straddles the two sides of the brain. Its brain mate, the hippocampus, recognizes and makes sense of patterns that arrive from the senses and puts those experiences in context.

Our hippocampus allows us to recognize that the bobcat is chasing the hare, and not us. It is the repository of dry facts, recording and fixing all the important details involved in a given event. The hippocampus notes the depth of the snow, the length and color of the bobcat's hair, the color of the sky, the temperature and weather, the sharpness of the claws, and the smell in the air. The amygdala then takes that information and flavors it with danger, grace, or amazement. The amygdala produces the emotional shade and hue of a situation, and the more stimulated the amygdala is, the more imprinted the memory will be.

After successfully avoiding the attack of the bobcat, the hare will remember the incident vividly, and when its hippocampus registers the same or similar conditions—snow depth, bobcat silhouette, feline movement, smell—the amygdala will jump to a conclusion based on the past memory. The amygdala functions as the emotional reservoir for memory and adds meaning to the facts the hippocampus provides.

In humans, not only fear but also laughter and joy erupt from the amygdala. If experiences are not given emotional weight by the amygdala, they become meaningless. Without an amygdala, individuals no longer recognize friends and loved ones and remain impassive in the face of suffering and pain in others. The amygdala and the other structures of the limbic system have been in the animal population for millions of years, and they function largely automatically, coordinated and mediated by the cortex in more evolved animals. The cortex sorts and compares experiences and provides more accurate and discriminating abilities.

We humans also have a neocortex, an additional layer of cells in our brains that allows us not only to sort and compare experiences, but also to think about them, and speculate about them, and imagine events based on the experiences we have already had. The neocortex sees nuance in experiences, analyzes components, and allows higher levels of emotional life not present in the amygdala, such as maternal care, ideological passion, and righteous indignation. The neocortex will still defer to the amygdala in emergencies, but during times of stability the higher brain develops complex ways of dealing with logical and emotional information to make better decisions and obtain richer meaning.

The wabi sabi way encourages subtle appreciation, which depends on this higher-level brain processing. But it also listens to the deepest messages from the amygdala, relying on that brain structure's emotional input to give objects and experiences meaning. The ability of the human mind to think about its thoughts and have feelings about its feelings makes us unique. When you find that you are overly stressed and suffer from too much sympathetic response to dangers or perceived dangers in the world around you, take these wabi sabi steps:

1. Think about how you can balance your sympathetic and parasympathetic responses. In the same way that the samurai warrior learned to balance his life of conflict and stress with the tranquility of the tea ceremony, modern-day citizens plying the dangerous waters of careers and social dynamics can balance their fights and flights with the rest and enjoyment of the journey. Include your parasympathetic needs in your daily organizer. Downtime is not time wasted; it is time spent restoring balance. Highlight the daily, seasonal, and environmental transitions, the equinoxes, solstices, and phases of the moon. Remember the advice of Aristotle, "Nature requires us not only to be able to work well, but also to idle well." Scrawl that quote across your calendar and block in idle time.

2. Recognize that the days of the winter months should be shorter, unless you live on the equator. Before electric lights were invented, people worked hard during the summer and less hard during the winter. Not only does the light from our overlit homes

and cities force us to work long hours all year long, it also hinders our ability to appreciate natural forms of nighttime light such as stars and fireflies. On a clear dark night in the countryside you can see about 2,500 celestial points of light with your warm naked eye. Stargazing is very relaxing. But if you look skyward in one of the suburbs of New York, for instance, you will be lucky to pick out 250 objects glowing in the quasi-dark, and if you live in a place like Manhattan you will probably only glimpse about fifteen dim smudges in the city overglow. Do yourself a favor and turn off the indoor lights, enjoy some beeswax candles, and make your bedroom a low-luminous sanctuary. Studies have shown that light striking the retina, even during sleep, can reduce production of melatonin, the hormone that helps regulate your circadian rhythms. Let your nights be dark and your days be light, but don't live in a never-ending artificial twilight.

3. To relax and counter the stress and anxiety of life in the complex and stimulating world of technology and commerce, wabi sabi individuals could take a lesson from the snowshoe hare. After an intense day at work or even at play, get off somewhere quiet and safe and allow that parasympathetic system to cut in. Soothe yourself with positive self-talk or ask someone close to you for a hug or a back rub or simply to listen while you talk about your day. As long as they offer reassuring comments in soft tones, your amygdala will recognize the gesture and allow the parasympathetic system to supply the proper therapy. Then return the favor.

4. Lie in a field.

How to lie in a field

The kind of field is important. Pick one that is clean and natural and preferably away from people and noise and artificial light. No cow patties for pillows, please. If you cannot find a meadow or field, a secluded corner of a city park or even your own backyard will do. The best time of year is late August, or whenever the grasses have dried and lost their seeds in your area. From evening to midnight is the best time to try this, because the ground is free of dew or excessive heat, and you don't have to contend with sunburn or headaches from the bright daytime light. The light of evening is rich with shadows and that warm mellow feel that highlights texture over color.

1. Wear a long-sleeved shirt and long pants to avoid prickles. Bring a handkerchief or towel to go under your head. Itching and scratching spoil the mood.

2. Inspect the ground for rocks, glass, or other debris that might be uncomfortable to lie on. Take your time; a good spot will be soft with dried plant matter and comfortable against your body. Feel yourself looking for the right spot and enjoy the intuitive moment when your body says, "Here."

3. When you have found a nice spot, orient yourself east to west, with your feet pointing east, where the sun comes up, and your head directed west, where it goes down. That way you align your body to the spin of the planet. Lie down with your arms and

legs slightly open and stare up at the sky. Let your joints and muscles go slack. Perhaps there will be some clouds to look at and some color from the setting sun. Just take it in as a gift for the eyes and wait for the stars to appear. If you need to sleep, let yourself drift off—it's okay; you probably need the rest. Your amygdala will wake you if there is danger, so don't worry.

4. Take a deep breath and smell the aromatic oils and woody scents of the dry grass stocks. Notice your breathing and let it come in and out of you, as it likes. Don't force it to be fast or slow, just notice how you feel as it changes. Ask your body to relax into the grass and imagine that when you breathe in, the grassy smell freshens and cleanses you.

5. Feel the ground under you. Imagine how Earth holds you as it revolves. If the sun is going down, you will get a sense that you are on the outside of that turning ball, watching new sky come into view as you turn with the planet. This is a lovely feeling, a reorientation from the normal sense that Earth is stationary and the sun moves. You are riding a great majestic rotation, a privileged passenger on the star liner Earth.

6. Feel your own weight on the ground and know that all the atoms in your body are responding in the same way as all the other atoms in the plants and trees around you, under the influence of mutual gravitation. If there are trees around you, contemplate their ability to stand up against this force. If there are only grass stocks and blades, notice how they push away from the effect of gravity.

7. Close your eyes and feel the pressure of the earth along the back of your body and your arms and legs. Think of how Earth is moving through space as it travels around the sun at an average speed of 67,000 miles per hour; then think that the solar system is traveling through space with the rest of the galaxy at around 140 miles per second. Pretty nice to be safely fixed on the surface with all that air above you to buffer any objects that might stray in front of you, right?

8. Think about the soil and rock underneath you. If you live where there is sandstone, there could be fossils beneath your body. If you live where there are deep layers of soil, imagine how many years of growth and decay contributed to that soil. Perhaps great glaciers scraped away the soil from some distant place and dropped it here, or maybe massive glaciers themselves grinding solid rock into silt and sediment made the sands and soils underneath you. Imagine how tall that glacier would be above you if it were still here. Maybe lava once flowed where you are now lying, or some other geologic activity. Feel how old Earth is. Remember that your body is made up of the molecules of the planet and plants and animals that grew on it.

9. Listen. You will hear the breeze moving in the trees or grass. Perhaps there is water in a stream burbling nearby, perhaps crickets rasping out their love songs in the hay. Bird song, the flutter of a little brown bat, the sound of your own breath in the relative silence.

10. Feel the freedom of not having to stand erect, and remember how many religions in the world pray on the ground in humble recognition of our smallness in comparison to the grandeur of existence. It is good to recognize that you depend on the planet, are inseparable from it. And it is good to know that in the entire world there is no one like you, that God, maybe, is looking at you here in the field taking time out to just be. Feel your dinner digesting inside you, giving you nutrients and energy so that your body can repair itself and restock its stores. Enjoy being renewed and thank your body for doing its job so faithfully.

If you can do this, if you can "rest" in nature and not worry about the "rest" of your life, you will be practicing wabi sabi. But if the world rushes into your field with you, if your worries and fears take a spot beside you in the grass, just smile and let them. Imagine them leaning back in the grass and looking at the stars. Imagine your boss and coworkers there with you, taking in the cool evening air. If your inner clock-watcher is chirping out the prerecorded message implanted in you from the culture of excess, "unproductive time is a waste of time," ask that little cuckoo bird to take a tumble in the hay beside you. Relaxation is not something you "get done." It is the opposite of doing; it is being.

Think about that hare and all the other animals that take time to heal, make time to lick their wounds in thought-neutral attention to the way of the parasympathetic rhythms. Imagine that hare resting beside you. Do what she does. Take the time to train your amygdala that lying in a field is para-time, time to let the tension leave your body. Imagine gravity pulling all the heaviness out of you. Imagine it sinking into the soil beneath you. When you get up, leave the weight of the world there in the grass. Leave your boss and coworkers relaxing in the growing darkness; let them return home by a different path. Go home alone without them.

The smell of flowers and the taste of plum pudding

The use of flowers in cooking is centuries old. Flowers add much pleasure to food, both in presentation and in flavor. From your herb garden you can select the flowers of rosemary, thyme, borage, marjoram, lovage, fennel, coriander, and chive. As garnishes on dishes with the same herbal bouquet, they add interest, beauty, and fun. A favorite summer recipe is peach and carrot soup with rosemary flowers scattered on the surface. Nasturtium, marigold, pansy, and chicory flowers can be used in salads along with rose petals, geranium petals, violas, and even day lily and hollyhock petals.

Even if you don't cook with them, bring flowers into your home. They mark the seasons and have been shown to improve health, just by being present in a room. Experts like Dr. Andrew Weil recommend that you bring flowers into your home on a daily basis, even when they are not in season. Wabi sabi wisdom will let you find what is right for you. One of the treasured times of year in our house is when the sweet peas first come into bloom. It seems to announce that summer has arrived. I love to watch Marilyn outside, collecting the pastel blooms in large bunches. We have them planted under our bedroom window so that on warm summer evenings the scent of them drifts in on the night breeze.

Rikyu stripped all unnecessary items from the tearoom, but he left a flower arrangement. He recommended, "arrange the flowers as they are in the field; in summer suggest coolness; in winter, warmth." The morning glory was used in the summer because its deep blue trumpet shape suggested a pool of water, and because morning glories open in the morning and evening, when the summer day is coolest, this association worked. Winter flowers like the Christmas cactus with its fiery red blooms bring summer warmth to the middle of the winter. All flowers, regardless of their season, remind us of the beauty of nature, and their short period of bloom instructs us to enjoy such beauty when it is available. Curled and wilted flowers need not be sad; they remind us that brilliant sexual displays (flowers are the plant's sex organs) are for a season and that fruit and seeds are the way of things. Dried fruit like raisins, prunes, blueberries, and cranberries can be eaten and remembered as the produce of nature's flowering.

I took a crumbling cookbook out recently to see if it had a traditional recipe for Christmas plum pudding. My Aunt Evelyn gave me the cookbook, which had been my grandmother's, kept safe in a plastic bag. Published in 1894 by E. A. Weeks & Company and written by one Miss E. Neil, the brittle and stained pages spilled out an assortment of clippings and handwritten recipes cut or copied by my grandmother long before I was born.

As a child I had always hated '60s-style plum pudding, dressed up with maraschino cherries and green cubes of questionable origin packed alongside the dark prunish objects I knew were not prunes, but raisins and currants in soggy porous cake, sticky and pungent with the aroma of alcohol.

Then, on my thirty-seventh Christmas, I observed with calloused resolve a dinner host preparing a plum pudding fresh from a tin, imported directly from Britain. The tin, at least, was nice to look at, but I dreaded the contents. My host lit the tin-shaped mass and placed it on the table, an eerie glowing treat, a thing of amusement as much as a dessert. Surprisingly, I found the taste interesting. It had been twenty-five years since I had tried to eat it, and I found it newly rich and filled with subtle flavors. I didn't eat a lot. Like pâté or caviar, too much would spoil the effect. What would be next, I wondered. Would I take a liking to fruitcake, the second most disappointing dessert of my childhood Christmas memories?

A mere two centuries old, the original plum puddings were filled with meat and fruit and generous amounts of beef tallow or suet. In 1843 Dickens wrote about Mrs. Cratchit bringing in a pudding "like a speckled cannon-ball, so hard and firm, blazing in half of half-a-quartern of ignited brandy, and bedight with Christmas holly stuck on top." Clearly the entertainment value has been part of its longtime success. In those days, "proper puddings" were prepared between July and October and aged in generous amounts of brandy. They were stirred by every member of the family, from east to west, never the other way, to symbolize the journey of the magi from the East to see the baby Jesus. Can there be a more wabi sabi food—one more evocative of process, tradition, and humble beauty? Grandma's cookbook called for, among other things, ¼ pound of citron, shred fine; 12 eggs; 2 grated nutmegs; 1 pound of butter; and 1 pound of suet—freed from strings and chopped fine. The prescribed cooking method: boiled in a cloth bag for 5 hours.

Inserted in the page was a clipped recipe that called for ¼ cup of fruit juice to replace the 1 cup brandy. Did my grandmother's Salvation Army sensibility cause her to look for alternatives to the alcohol? Elsewhere in the book was a recipe for devil's food cake, made with honey instead of sugar. I love the fact that this old recipe simply gave the list of ingredients, noting specifically the substitutable amounts of sweetener and assuming that everyone would know how to put the ingredients together properly. In a world of fast food and ever faster eating, it is good to slow down and savor some of these old-time flavors.

Nostalgic tastes and smells bring your attention to food in sharp and clear moments of appreciation. Re-creating those recipes can be a deliberate attempt to bring about that appreciation. Your senses bring you to the real world, and when you pay attention to your senses, you become aware of how substantial things are. You taste the layers. You intuitively feel the complexity, but have you ever tried to describe the taste of a subtle flavor? Direct sensations are hard to put into words. The very act of describing a taste or smell forces your awareness onto it, focuses the experience with a linguistic lens. And in a world of myriad distractions, focus can be hard to maintain. Focus allows you to burrow down into simple pleasures and mine out nuggets of meaning. As the Zen master Dogen said, "attainment of the Way can only be achieved with one's body." Religious practices are not designed for you to achieve awareness; awareness is inherent in the practices. Wabi sabi points to direct experience of nature as awareness itself. When we are eating a plum pudding or smelling a flower, or conversely smelling a plum pudding or eating a flower, we are aware. This is the path.

Paddles and smooth stones

As the bobcat and hare illustration revealed, stress is a part of nature, but fortunately we humans occupy top place in the food chain, so when we enter a forest the creatures we encounter are usually the ones that scurry away in fear. No stronger advice can be given on the wabi sabi path than to spend time in nature. Once you know how safe it really is, connection with nature is the single most effective way to calm your mind and be aware.

Three simple elements of nature work strange magic on the nervous system to calm and restore harmony. They are lapping water, rustling foliage, and smooth stones. Four places afford this combination: the streamside, the riverside, the lakeside, and the oceanside. These locations, where water and land and air all meet, where wind ruffles both the leaves and the waves, produce the textured sounds of natural motion, the random noise that uniquely mends our fractured soul. I have found that taking advantage of that sweet spot of nature, the shoreline, is best achieved from the water in a small paddled craft. The market offers many kinds of canoes and kayaks and all of them allow you to cruise along the fractal shore of any body of water. The act of paddling is rich with mystery. The paddle slides into the water and by pushing the water one way, you go the other. Floating quietly, only the sound of the paddle and the small curl of wake off the side of the craft, you experience the wonder of buoyancy, of moving smoothly across a liquid surface because of the shape of the hull of your craft.

The surface of the water holds many pleasures. The way it curves up to meet objects, including the legs of water striders. The way it slides over itself in sheets when it is very calm but moving slightly. The way it returns to calmness when it is disturbed. The way a rock pierces it when thrown from your hand, and the way the ripples create a target after the fact so that you hit a bull's-eye every time.

The water itself when looked into near shore accentuates the colors of the stones. Retrieved from the water, they dry and grow dull, but under its magic surface they are radiant and rich. I think the water's motion makes it so effective in stimulating the relaxation response. The slight bobbing of the boat, the way waves slide up a beach, the way the water swirls around your paddle creating eddies and bubbles and, at night on the ocean, swirls of bioluminescence to mirror the stars.

Are you one of those people who pocket stones when you are at the shore? Most people have found a stone at least one time in their life that they brought home just to have with them. For many years I had a little basket of them on my desk. There is something about the smooth surface of a well-worn stone that calms us. Worry stones, some people call them, because by rubbing them we keep worry at bay. The smooth appearance and soft surface of weatherworn stones seem to have an effect on the amygdala. What better way to stimulate the parasympathetic system than to go for a walk in nature and bring home a smooth stone? When you look for stones, don't turn the activity into a treasure hunt; that is a sympathetic activity. Instead, let the universe guide you to the stone by its surreptitious means. Suspend your need to find a stone, and let the stone find you.

Archery and intuition

There are different kinds of paradoxes. There are linguistic ones like my favorite: "All general statements are false." A paradox, through its strange Möbius-strip reality, can take the mind to a level of understanding beyond mere logic and deduction. There are paradoxes in physics, like the Möbius strip itself (a plane with only one side and one edge) or the way that light is either a particle or wave, depending on how you measure it. In archery you sometimes have a contest to see who will get the highest score, but master archers compete primarily with themselves. This paradoxical contest is what some athletes call their personal best, but it can go beyond a simple increase in skill level over time.

In Japan, archery and swordsmanship are two practices of Zen. To be a master archer is to be a Zen master. Zen archery reworks the existence of competition so that it connects to the mystical unity of everything, releasing the mimetic temptation to sort the world into "them and us" or "me and you." Instead, it embraces the existence of only I, the I that connects to the earth and environment so that when I aim at the target, I aim at myself. Hitting the target is a reflection of how well I have connected with that unity. Like the stone thrown into the water creating its own bull's-eye, the arrow on the bow becomes a precursor to a bull's-eye that will be. The final step in Zen archery is to remove the "I" altogether so that only the shot remains, making itself.

Here is how a person becomes a Zen archer. First, the student must learn the art. Mastery of any art requires obtaining technical knowledge and then transcending technique. An instructor teaches a person to hold a bow, notch an arrow, and pull and release it toward a target. In Japan this is done by the mimetic method. The master demonstrates, students imitate, and the master then watches the students practice and gives more demonstration. Of course, the bow and arrow are only a means for something that can also happen with tea, or flower arranging, or gardening, or any other activity.

In fact, to the Zen master every activity is a possibility to awaken. Zen is sometimes called the everyday mind, which is simply "sleeping when tired and eating when hungry." It is shooting the arrow when it is time to shoot it. It is doing what comes naturally in the rhythms of the day. If you think too much about it, it spoils the moment. If you cease to eat while eating, sleep while sleeping, walk while walking, sit while sitting, it is gone. Jesus said to emulate children in this regard, and Zen masters point to the childlike mind that does what it needs to when it needs to. It is spontaneous action without unnecessary forethought. This is not to say that thinking cannot be a Zen activity; it can, as long as it is not trying to be something else. A Zen master would say that the best thing to do is to think while thinking.

After the student learns basic techniques, after she sets up the rhythm, the student settles into the tension of the bow and string, waiting for the shot to take itself. If the "I" is removed, the shot occurs on its own. During this period of training, much emphasis is placed on proper breathing and the release of desire and ego.

Then, after months or years of practice, the actions of the art are so familiar that the student becomes aware of the inner meaning of the actions. Intention is lost in the commitment to do the actions regardless of the outcome.

Illustrations are used to hint at the way, such as snow falling off a bamboo leaf or a fly being caught in a spider's web. Neither the bamboo leaf, nor the fly, nor the spider intend for the action to take place. In this way the archer releases the arrow like the snow that slides off the leaf. The leaf does not decide to let the snow off, nor does it act to loose the snow. In the same way the fly does not decide to hit the web and the spider does not intend for that particular fly to be caught. The fly and the spider and the snow and the bamboo are all part of a whole that works together. In this final state, the archer obtains enlightenment.

Wabi sabi relaxation is the relaxation of that final state. Only one who is himself or herself wabi sabi can understand this wabi sabi way. The only way to experience it is to practice it in such a way that the experience is not the goal. If you are tempted to gain the wabi sabi way by just thinking about it, or just wanting it, it will not happen. Relaxation occurs when you stop trying, stop striving, and stop the stimulation that keeps you in stress. The amygdala responds to a lack of stimulation and produces the parasympathetic response; it cannot be forced or made to happen quickly. Quickness is a characteristic of the sympathetic system. At the end of the day you may find that what you were waiting for was the end of waiting. When that occurs you will have found the wabi sabi way.

Eight
Wabi sabi
in the garden

gives advice

while I dig the hole

neighbor's three-year-old boy

EAST SOOKE PARK on a calm Saturday afternoon. The wave-eroded rocks are warm, otters play in the kelp offshore, and Marilyn and I are eating sandwiches. We sit in a grove of stunted *Pinus contorta* trees 'so small and twisted that they hug the ground around our knees. Their Latin name pretty much tells it all, con-torted pines. The gnarled shapes of these tiny trees, their trunks like paralyzed pythons, strain across the rock and cover the fissured slope behind us. It is clear that for most of the year storms pummel this coast. And powerful storms they must be. Some of the trunks on these miniature trees are as big around as my arm, but the foliage is concentrated in tight little bundles on short stubby limbs.

Tree experts agree that this is a slow-growing species. One-hundred-year-old trees may have trunks less than 2 inches in diameter, depending on the conditions. They grow thicker and taller in bogs, but on these sloped coastal exposures they hunch against the rock for protection. The stone around them is smooth and scalloped and the bark on the trees is thick and armorlike. No sign points out these marvels, and no fences keep people back. The park's informal trail rambles along the high ground, and in one place it slices through a particularly dense clump of these wild bonsai. Twisted and bleached trunk stubs end abruptly in neat saw cuts with hardened droplets of faded amber pitch. The sacrifice of these few specimens, in clearing the trail, channels the traffic away from the rest. Park visitors can still climb out onto the exposed coastal rock, if they want, and stroll among the ancient pines like Gulliver among Lilliputian trees.

Up and down the shore hundreds of scraggly little clusters contain the shore pines and other hardy evergreens: ground juniper, Rocky Mountain juniper, arbutus, and the odd Douglas fir, all of them stunted and shaped by their harsh environment. Local homeowners point out the value of *Pinus contorta* for the yuletide season. They harvest the most upright specimens of the twisted trees that grow outside the park boundaries and use them for Christmas trees. They prize the trees for their tightly clustered foliage and intriguing shapes, their aromatic quality. By sawing off these shoreline soldiers to grace their holiday festivities, celebrants demonstrate the great power and desirability of wabi sabi trees.

Bonsai education

Most cultures frown upon the collection of wild trees and many governments legislate against it. But areas near human habitation have been surveyed for wild bonsai, and the prized and random treasures found there have been carefully dislodged and carried away. Some collectors fear that if they don't collect the specimens, someone else will. In certain regions of China, young people demonstrate the passage into adulthood by their ability to find a wild specimen from a remote and inaccessible place and bring it safely home. They act out a sort of quest for imperfection. Wild bonsai are, in some ways, the Holy Grail of the East. And they are a noticeably wabi sabi Grail.

Collectors find that transporting these trees from the wild to the garden fails more often than they would like, however. The fact that these trees are old and small gives away the less than romantic reality that they live where they live on the thinnest advantage, trading height and symmetry for prolonged existence. When a tree hovers on the edge of survival, uprooting it and bringing it home can be the final blow that kills it. Not to say that all bonsai collecting is a bad idea. Farmer's fields often harbor stunted trees that have been pruned repeatedly by cows and other farm animals. The farmer might welcome the tenacious invaders' removal from his field. Rubbish heaps and fallen-down walls often support unwanted specimens, as do hedges and building sites. One bonsai master tells of rescuing a tree from an old courtyard wall only hours before the wrecking ball destroyed the whole area. Such saved trees enhance any collection and leave no pang of guilt for removing them from their original habitat.

Contorted pines have adapted to live in harsh environments, taking the abuse of weather and waves as a fact of life. Sometimes only the wind assaults these trees, like at East Sooke Park. The howling winds bend every shoot of new growth, every branch of any substance; they either snap off or follow the line of least resistance. Most snap off. And at each break more shoots grow, smaller and less advancing, until mats of foliage form so tightly that each needle and branch braces against numerous others, forming in their proximity a whole that can stand against the onslaught. These trees do not exactly thrive; but they do survive. I have seen the wind buffet them. The small bonsai twist like crazy brooms in a gale, anchored to the rocks and at the same time sweeping the rocks clean. Their anchoring system is tough. The Nisga'a people of the Pacific Northwest used the gnarly roots of the contorted pine to make rope.

The bristlecone pines of the Great Basin in the western United States grow so slowly that they have adapted needles that can remain on the tree for twenty to thirty years. These trees are Earth's oldest living inhabitants, having shuffled into existence around the time of the pyramids. It is not just wind, but snow and lightning and animals and bitter conditions that prune the foliage and shape the trunks. Regardless of the species, be it West Coast contorted pine or Colorado bristlecone pine, or any of the thousands of trees that eke out their living in the outbacks of every continent, what these natural treasures have in common is their expression of wabi sabi. They are the quintessential examples. Humble battle-worn sentinels in the struggle to remain, they testify to the truth that harsh environment builds character.

Newcomers to the art of bonsai often think that they have to replicate this harshness in order to create trees of value. But harshness is not necessary. Simple practices such as pruning the roots at the right time of year encourages more roots to grow more densely. This means the trees can be planted in smaller containers. Special soil is added to further encourage the process. Wiring the branches and careful, regular pruning produce the same visual effect I admire in the East Sooke trees.

The art of bonsai is one of the most effective ways to craft a wabi sabi element in your garden. Practicing bonsai has taught me that wabi sabi isn't just about imperfection. Imperfection alone can be ugly, but the right kind of imperfection can be beautiful. Chipping a cup on purpose will not make it wabi sabi. A wabi sabi cup is simply one that is made more beautiful for having been chipped.

Prune and nurture

These words adorn the mantel of a stone fireplace in the home of a wealthy family: "If your heart is cold, my fire cannot warm you." This concept is important for anyone considering crafting his or her world toward wabi sabi. Adding an expensive stone fireplace or purchasing expensive bonsai trees, or tattooing a wabi sabi mark on your body, or wearing a wabi sabi sweater, or painting your house in wabi sabi colors will not, by itself, change your heart. Turning to a wabi sabi art form when your heart is still attached to the world of competition and greed may provide some balance, but it will ultimately turn the art into another possession, another plant in your garden, another thing you own, unless you first nurture your inner garden, the growing center of your life.

If you are committed to being natural and authentic, if your heartbeat has become attuned to the rhythm of the seasons, the percussion of rain and wind, then a garden can be an expression of who you are, and because you are authentic, it will be, too. When you garden, you enter into a partnership with nature to produce beauty. Shiro Nakane, in his book *In The Japanese Garden*, says, "Building a garden is like painting on a three-dimensional canvas." And you paint yourself into the picture. By gardening, you become a gardener, a person who works to make things grow.

While it is true that harshness produces beauty both in the painful procedure of receiving a tattoo and in the tortured life of a desert tree, gardening is not about suffering. Suffering alone does not create beauty in you or in plants. Not all tattoos are nice to look at, not all wastelands tug at our hearts, and not all gardens are wabi sabi. One of the secrets of nature is that the sheer volume of trees in all the forests of all the diverse conditions on the planet will mean that some particular specimens will stand out. But they stand out against the background of less remarkable trees that make up the bulk of the forest. Herein lies the secret to a wabi sabi garden: the background is as important as the fore-ground; the unremarkable has value as a backdrop for the remarkable.

In order for bonsai trees to be beautiful and to stay beautiful, they must be tended. Warm human hands must water bonsai daily during the growing season, and bed them snuggly into shelter for the winter. A sensitive human heart must look for the potential in a bonsai and guide the growth of limbs and branches with wire and pruning. Fertilizer must be added, new pots must be selected, and soil must be replaced regularly to keep the bonsai looking its best and developing as it should. The analogy is pretty obvious. It is attention and care that grow a successful bonsai and also a successful human.

Right now there is a rush to find the next feng shui that will offer solutions for saving hollow lives. One reason feng shui has been popular is because it has something to say about wealth.

But people have put fountains in their wealth corner and nothing has happened. Their lives remained poor and bitter. There are no easy ways to transform pain into patina. Those folk who garnered pretty pines for their Christmas season eventually dumped the dried remains on the curb along with everyone else. Wabi sabi is not quick. It celebrates slowness, timelessness, mellowing. It allows mistakes and promises recovery from those mistakes. This is the only wisdom it has. Acceptance of pain as a part of life lies near the heart of wabi sabi, but this does not mean we should impose pain intentionally.

A bonsai artist looks for the character that lies in the response to hardship and shapes that response into beauty. She employs careful sight that scans the bonsai for buds, down near the bark line, seeing where the growth will be, imagining what the tree will look like in ten years, in twenty years, after the artist has died. In this way your life will open like a small cell that opens into the larger monastery. You can craft this kind of life in the careful and thoughtful selecting, adjusting, and arranging of small things now that will have lasting effects over time.

When a heart loves wabi sabi, when you internalize the admonition to trust the beauty, a desire to grow life around that value will naturally develop. Wabi sabi is not about fortress building, creating a safe place from the storms of life. Neither is it about escape into the wilderness, away from the rough city with all its smog and chaos. Wabi sabi is about making sure the buds will form and waiting patiently for the seasons to change.

Japanese gardens

Like the tea ceremony, bonsai is simple. Yet it can take many years or a lifetime to learn. It is growing trees and plants in small, carefully chosen pots to create a wabi sabi feeling in those who view them. Bonsai are stories, replicas, impressions of the kinds of trees that exist in nature that move us with their ancient beauty. A work of art can express Zen through seven characteristics. The art of bonsai has long recognized these characteristics and incorporated them. They are asymmetry, simplicity, austere sublimity, naturalness, subtle profundity, freedom from attachment, and tranquility.

Asymmetry

Unlike the perfectly square, spherical, or other modular forms of contemporary culture, bonsai growers aspire to a natural arrangement produced by the efforts of growth and life balanced out by the states of gravity and decay. The tree reveals this in the lack of an obvious center of gravity.

The Chinese only use geometric lines and shapes to indicate the presence of human influence in a garden. They reflect the presence of an observer. Human corners and edges stand in contrast to the flowing lack of delineation in foliage. The edges of the bonsai pot in the same way contrast to the organic form of the bonsai tree.

Japanese houses use lines to draw the eye toward the garden, and also to frame a view of the garden or indicate an area of transition. In this way the symmetry of human buildings become windows on the wider and bigger world of asymmetrical nature. The garden is, after all, not intended to be a wild place void of human attention. It is a harmonious place in which a person can feel that he or she belongs.

Simplicity

It is possible to make a garden into a burden. Elaborate arbors and fences, demanding specialty plants, and labor-intensive lawns and borders, while beautiful, can make a garden a distraction, a place to spend effort and energy in a seamless continuation of the busyness of life in the world of excess. If you want your garden to be a place of peace, design it in such a way that it allows you to be in it without always having to work in it. Gardeners who understand this choose the size of their gardens carefully and decide where they will put their efforts. It is better to tend a few chosen bonsai trees that give pleasure than to work doggedly in a garden overrun with weeds and grass.

By using native plants, carefully chosen stones, drip irrigation, and appropriate and low-maintenance groundcover, you can make your garden look attractive with only moderate upkeep. Many bonsai growers use brick and stone patios, gravel borders, and landscaping fabric to eliminate or minimize lawns, annual beds, and edging. This design draws the eye across the neutral areas to the focal points that are the bonsai themselves.

Austere sublimity

The shore pines measure their growth in decades or even centuries, and so invest in thick trunks and strong roots to withstand the wind and waves. When attempting to tell this story in your garden, present a tree in a way that reflects its natural cousins growing wild in their environment. The art is in achieving the look of a mature tree without it looking like it has been manipulated into a mere copy, or "ideal" tree.

The bonsai should evoke a small smile of recognition, a wrinkling around the eyes as one part of the specimen draws your focus, then the other. Jarring shapes and unbalanced limbs cause the eye to stop abruptly or flit away. Subtle transitions and gradations, and clean but intricate patterns, on the other hand, satisfy the eye and calm the mind. By gazing on the small tree you can bring an ancient and distant cliff edge into imagination where such a specimen might grow. The "treeness" of the tree, the hints of hostile and severe landscape, captured in the shape and bearing of the bonsai lead the mind to grander scales, seeds the mind with the essence of a rugged coastline or a windswept mountain. The tree that can survive there is sublime and noble. These austere echoes of wild grandeur are what cause that smile, that search of the eye for the source of such a magnificent feeling from such a small object.

Naturalness

The bonsai plant is a living thing. The process of growing it to look old, while keeping it small, involves finding what will produce that look by observing naturally stunted trees in the wild and by experimenting with techniques learned over the years by bonsai artists. There was a time when bonsai plants became almost stylized into plastic caricatures of trees. Like Platonic incarnations of "the perfect tree" they failed to capture the essence of natural beauty because they were conforming to an ideal of beauty.

Part of the appeal of a gnarled and twisted bonsai is that it demonstrates that natural beauty is imperfect and that imperfection cannot be perfected. Working with the tree itself, looking closely at the way the tree wishes to be, will guide the gardener to that same state that the archer practices to achieve. In this way the bonsai artist simply allows the tree to take shape. The work of the artist is to find the shape it should be as the seasons progress.

The other aspect of naturalness that needs to be considered is "fit." A bonsai tree should look like it belongs. Are they out of place, out of balance, or conversely, lost in the grandeur of an ornate garden? With the overall size of a garden, my rule of thumb is that small areas work best. These can be joined by passages to other small areas, giving the impression of outdoor rooms. Unless you have a great deal of time to spend on a large garden, I suggest you focus on a few small areas. Attention to a small area can produce more satisfying results and allow you time to "be" in the garden without worrying about "working" in the garden. The *tsuboniwa,* or courtyard garden, is a great model to consider when thinking about size and effort.

Subtle profundity

The Chinese have a proverb, "Life begins on the day you start a garden." The outer garden, in this way, can come to reflect your inner garden. Each bonsai tree, through the forms and patterns you develop, can reflect profundity in subtle and varied ways. The Japanese successfully capture the heart of Zen in their careful placement of stone, walls, water, and trees. You can do the same for your own deep beliefs.

Freedom from attachment

The third Noble Truth of Buddhism is that suffering ceases when you free your mind from attachment to things and from the need to control them. When the mind experiences full freedom, or "nonattachment," it is called Nirvana. The Eight-Fold Path is designed to help achieve this nonattachment. The idea of wabi sabi can help you accept the fact that nothing is ultimately yours and all your tools and resources will pass on to someone else when you are gone. Your garden can be part of this gesture. Planting a tree is a wabi sabi gift of generational proportion. Even though you may not live to enjoy its mature beauty and shade, others will.

At first glance you might think a garden is about attachment. Roots grip rock and soil, moss hangs on to branches, and vines cling to arbors with tendril efficiency. But this kind of attachment does not cause pain. Ownership and possession cause pain, and almost everything about a garden teaches the folly of this. The gentle flower blossom gives away its beauty, its scent, and softness. Seedpods burst their bounty and sparrows and squirrels alike enjoy them. The neighbor on her way to work receives the gift of beauty from your garden, be it a full-sized suburban lot or a window box in the heart of the city.

What's more, the garden doesn't only demonstrate freedom from attachment; it creates it, in you. Not only do plants and trees grow in directions that are unpredictable, and therefore outside your control, but the garden also presents itself to you without distinctions, or dissociations. You see it first as one multihued mosaic of nature, one expansive growth happening beyond your control. Then you see the individual leaves and flowers, you differentiate the separate plants and bushes. Then you integrate the parts back into the garden and appreciate it whole again. The Japanese garden, with its emphasis on shape and form, draws the eye always to a new sight, a new angle, increasing awareness of just how organic the world is, how layered and shaded, how subtle. This effect of seeing both the big undifferentiated garden and also the differentiated leaves and flowers works like a Zen koan to tease your mind.

It's true that we speak of owning a garden, but most gardeners realize eventually that the garden owns them, too. This is the point at which you experience freedom from attachment. If you can let go of your preconceived notion of how your garden should be, you can start to come into partnership with nature, letting the garden itself inform you as to how it should be pruned, arranged, improved. A wabi sabi garden is rather wild, rather out of control. A wabi sabi gardener does not have a heavy hand, but instead works to find natural harmony in the elements. If you can approach the garden in this way it will reward you with lesson after lesson. The lesson of bonsai, for example, is that a single plant can contain the same wisdom. It is a special honor to receive a bonsai tree from a great old master gardener. In passing a bonsai tree like a wabi sabi baton to the next generation, the gardener submits to the pulse and rhythm of nature and the grand array of human connections within it. Many Japanese gardens are small, some existing only in pots on an eighth-floor balcony, but as long as they are allowed to be, to follow the natural patterns of growth, they will remind you of the value in freedom from attachment.

Critics of Buddhism have contended that attachments are what make life meaningful, that to say "I'm very attached to you" expresses love and affection. Wabi sabi people know that love and affection exist apart from the attachment, that you can love something and find it beautiful, without having to own or manip- ulate it, without having to make it your possession.

Japanese homes are designed to minimize the sense of sepa- ration from nature. Large openings look out on the garden and large open patios and verandas join the garden to the house. The garden is for everyone, a place to bring your guests, a wabi sabi part of your environment that they will enjoy.

Tranquility

A garden is a retreat you keep close to you. It is a room out of doors that you fill with the things a house finds hard to hold. It is the place you plant things, the place you compost things, it is the place you go to when the buzz of the electric world gets too much for you. The garden, regardless of what you do or do not do to it, will of its own accord offer you tranquility. It is in the blades and stems and leaves and petals, and it unfolds within you when you turn to these elements in the garden. The wise gardener, or bonsai artist, simply makes room for it to expand, looks for ways to let it be, knowing that it cannot be obtained, purchased, or built. It can only be grown.

Rain on leaves

Those who are used to the bold flavors of other cultures have sometimes described Japanese food as bland. The fish, rice, and vegetables are often visually appealing and texturally interesting, but can nevertheless seem a little underwhelming when it comes to flavor. To appreciate the Japanese palate is to become sensitive to subtlety. Just as the Japanese linger over the faint perfume of plum blossoms while passing by the bold smell of lilies, they also savor the subtle distinctions between different kinds of fresh fish in sushi while politely avoiding heavily spiced combination dishes.

Because of Japan's unique climate and grand diversity of seasonal produce, the sheer variety of natural ingredients has taken the place that spices occupy in other cultures. Classic Japanese dishes highlight the natural ingredients, not the sauces or dips that accompany them. The fineness of a person's palate is tested with subtle varieties of tea and food. In the same way, Japanese gardens are not showcases of exotic and brightly colored flowers. Instead, the multiple shades of green, brown, and gray draw the eye to shape and texture, and use brighter colors only as accents.

One morning while walking in the rain, I came upon an opening in the forest where ivy was growing in thick patches along the ground and also up the trunks of many trees. The particular shape and size of the ivy leaves under the intense barrage of large raindrops filled the grove with a sound that stopped me in my tracks. It was, when I focused on it, a sort of crisp splatting noise, not unlike the sound of rain on a tent roof. But unlike rain on a tent roof, there was not just one resonating fabric but, instead, many individual resonating leaves, each with a slightly different tone and volume. It was language pouring off the leaves, creating a mist of meaning in the saturated light. The message was difficult to discern, subtle and old, and it goes on talking even as I confess my difficulty in translation. It was a proclamation, a many-throated salutation, shouting like a trout underwater. I stood listening. Leaking into my mind came a small impression, a hint like a green caress, that something beyond language was with me, filling me with priceless sound, informing me with dollarless depth, drenching me in free time. The wild talk of anonymous gifts. Wet bullets of irrational talk ricocheting into tranquility. And if I listened for the rest of my life, I knew, I would never hear it all.

Nine
Wabi sabi creativity

swerve curve

behind the darting Chickadee

the line my mind makes

THE INFLUENCE OF WABI SABI on creativity begins with a simple premise: Do only what is necessary to convey what is essential. In bonsai and also in haiku, you prune and trim what is nonessential in an attempt to shorten the distance between the observer and the observed. You carefully eliminate elements that distract from the essential whole, elements that obstruct or obscure. This may be the fundamental effect of wabi sabi on art. Art trimmed in this way is slender and precise, like a blade of grass. Clutter, bulk, and erudition confuse perception and stifle comprehension, whereas simplicity allows clear and direct attention.

When a haiku succeeds, its subject comes into focus in the same way a subject does under a microscope or through binoculars when the focus knob achieves the correct lens distance. A sudden dimming of peripheral light and noise and a deepening of inner stillness brings that profound and subtle way of seeing into things we call insight. At that moment, an important corollary event occurs inside: self falls away. The attitude of focusing outside of yourself and onto the natural world frees you from the snares of self-absorption. Haiku writers embrace this outward-looking view, making this style of poetry one of the most widely read and written forms today.

Besides this focus, haiku has three other deeply appealing aspects. The first is the "haiku moment" that occurs in real time, in real life, that occasionally sparks the second aspect, a bright state of desire that bursts in on some haiku moments and that the poem often captures. The third is the mechanics of the poem, the way that elements, words, and lines work to re-create the feeling of the haiku moment or sometimes a wholly new feeling that reveals something bigger than the moment itself.

The power of haiku moments

Haiku moments happen all the time, all around you, even in crowds. You may not always see and appreciate them because they require an eye trained to look past the busy events that camouflage them. When you do see them, they will most likely be fleeting products of coincidence, or the juxtaposition of random elements, but they will catch your attention and make you smile, or frown, or ponder. Once you start to see them, they will become easier to see and will enrich your life, deepen it, and deepen your connection to the events that contain them. You may desire to write them down, to share them with others. The effort honors the moment, refocuses it, and takes it to a different level, the level of poetry.

This occurred last year when I took my sons to a Remembrance Day ceremony. The streets had been blocked off for the Veterans' Parade and people lined the sidewalks. We watched the procession and then the laying of wreaths at the cenotaph. Then, a strange juxtaposition occurred that struck me as significant and I wrote this haiku:

Cenotaph on Remembrance Day

war planes fly low

then two seagulls

Unlike journalism, which seeks to summarize and explain big complex stories, haiku poems present simple, small images with little or no explanation, trusting other humans to put together the images and find the meaning. The idea is to capture the moment in one breath, a whisper in the ear of the reader, a bright clear sparkle from the moment itself.

Imagine that you have a great day at work, one in which everything goes right and you feel like celebrating. You invite a friend to have dinner with you at a restaurant you have heard has good food, and you are ravishingly hungry by the time the food arrives, steaming and sizzling. Your mouth waters and you smell that smell you have been hoping to smell, the aroma of a meal cooked just the way you like it. The first bite unleashes your neurons in a flood of satisfaction, pleasure, and attention. "Oh, this is good," you mumble to your friend, with your mouth full. Your friend smiles, enjoying the meal with you. You take another bite and all of a sudden you can't get enough; you eat passionately, each chew delivering texture, flavor, sumptuous happy feelings. Then, you lean back and take in the moment, your friend, the restaurant, and the meal. You move from rapture to satisfaction.

That same satisfaction renews later in the evening when you comment on the meal. "Wasn't that a good meal?" you say, and your friend says, "The best." You resolve to eat there the next night, and you do, and the food is good, but not as good as you remember. After a week you go again, hoping for that first experience, but it doesn't happen. The food is still tasty, but not as delicious as you hoped, wished, imagined it would be. What has happened is that you have tasted something other than the meal, the sweet poison of the false infinite. It was sweet because you perceive it as good. But it makes you sick when you try to get it again and you don't succeed. And it is a false infinite because even though you want to have it again and again, forever, you cannot recapture that first moment of pleasure.

This example shows that we can become overly attached to a particular moment. When we experience heightened sensation as a result of having an ideal day, followed by a thoroughly satisfying meal, we start to long for that experience again. But unless the day is played out the same way, unless a mental state is achieved that is very similar to the one in memory, we will not find the same delight. It might be close, we may still enjoy it, but the longing for that memorable meal will remain. We think we want the same meal and we want to ensure that we will be able to have it in the future, forever in fact, if we could, and there is a pang of fear, a jab of doubt that we will have that experience again, so that against our strongest wishes the meal that seemed so sweet reveals a hidden poison.

The world is full of gluttons. Those who eat too much, drink too much, have too much sex, too much coffee, too much exercise. People buy too much music, too much insurance, too much house, too much car, too much vacation, too much clothing, too much makeup, too much everything. Humans grasp after pleasure. If we really believed that life would provide us with everything we desire, we would not claw after it; but we believe in shortage, in loss, and make absence of the pleasure more real than the pleasure itself. Pleasure, after all, is only a temporary state. We cannot live in a state of perpetual pleasure. Our nerves would become overstimulated, overworked, and the ability to experience the pleasure would stop.

We need a way to relive a moment in a different way. Haiku takes the moment and elevates it beyond gluttony, beyond fear of losing it, beyond anxiety about having enough. It lets the moment go, by moving it into art. Here is how that moment might look when complete in a haiku:

eyes closed to savor the meal

for dessert

Marilyn's smile

If the haiku works, the memory of the meal is no longer tinged with regret that you cannot experience it again. Instead, concentration moves from the meal to the abiding presence of the friend. In this way memory teases out the golden threads of the moment and weaves them into a blanket of content, of contentment. To continue grasping after the pleasure when it has passed forestalls or even destroys the greater pleasure that is found in its completion as art. The artistic expression of pleasure gives it new substance. Masaoka Shiki, a key voice in the reformation of haiku 100 years ago, said that the minimum requirement for a haiku was that it was "worth keeping as a record of the day." Remind yourself of this as you write and use the little poems to mark your days and seasons.

The deep longing of wabi sabi

Literary critics first used the word *sabi* to describe a kind of beauty captured in twelfth-century Japanese poetry. It is a beauty that aches with melancholy longing, a beauty of unseen selfless deeds, unrecognized acts of goodness, and a piercing beauty of moments that have passed and will not come again.

C. S. Lewis, the famous writer and Oxford theologian of the last century, described three moments in his life that contained this kind of longing. The first was a memory of his brother's miniature garden, triggered one summer day while he stood by a flowering currant bush. The second was a troubling shock while reading Beatrix Potter's *Squirrel Nutkin*, which contained the "Idea of Autumn," and the third was a blast of longing while casually reading a poem of Longfellow's about the death of a Nordic god.

Lewis explained that his longing was for something reflected in, yet beyond, these triggering experiences. The longing he felt was instantly itself desirable. He wanted to feel it again. Lewis described the longing as intense and surprising. He compared it to Milton's description of the "enormous bliss" of Eden. Yet at the same time, it was an unhappiness similar to grief. When you experience wabi sabi like Lewis did, you yearn for a desire deeper than your daily desires. A desire ephemeral and out of our control, that comes on you when we least expect it. The Japanese call this thing longed for *musō* the "unchanging formlessness behind all phenomena." Lewis concluded, "The form of the desired is in the desire." Bashō expressed it when he wrote:

> *even in Kyoto*
>
> *hearing the cuckoo's call*
>
> *I long for Kyoto*

At first, perhaps Bashō's poem seems like a riddle. If he is in Kyoto, why does the cuckoo's call stir a longing for Kyoto? Bashō realized, like many others, that the desirable quality of a thing or place may often not be the thing itself, but all that it represents. Kyoto was a beautiful city where the arts flourished, but it was all that Kyoto represented that Bashō longed for. He wrote this haiku to share the longing and the insight it brought. In a way it is a poem to see if others share, know, or recognize what he experienced.

C. S. Lewis's description of a haiku moment is important because he wrote from outside the haiku tradition. He gives independent witness to the power of the haiku moment and reveals that the moments themselves are universal, as likely to occur in the life of an Oxford scholar as in the life of a master Japanese *haijin*, like Bashō. Not all haiku moments are as intense as Lewis or Bashō described and not all haiku will translate that deep longing to others, but the fact that we can read Lewis or Bashō and connect with their feelings reinforces the value of writing haiku or expressing the haiku moment in other creative ways.

The rules and disciplines of haiku

Some haiku poets, or *haijin*, place the haiku moment above the traditional forms for capturing the moment. They justify deviation from established rules by appealing to creative freedom.

In contrast to this are those poets who, having experienced beauty and power in the established forms, seek to re-create the haiku moment through proven and established means. The danger of the first approach is that it can stumble on sentimentality, abstraction, morality, or one of the hundreds of other lesser temptations for writers unfamiliar with the disciplines of the form. The danger of the second approach is that it can become myopic and exclusionistic, including mimetically motivated judgments that stifle and constrain the creative spirit.

While driving home from a friend's house recently I noticed a situation that made me smile and wish to write a haiku. It was a hot day, near the end of September, and on one stretch of the sunny highway a young woman sat on the curb in a patch of shade, perspiration clearly visible shining on her face. I wrote:

dry September road

lone shadow across both lanes

she sits down in it

This poem is a technically correct haiku; it has three lines, has the familiar 5-7-5 syllable structures, contains a seasonal word, is written in the present tense, does not have a reference to the author, has a natural setting, and has an "aha!" realization that she has chosen to sit there because it is in the shade. After some consideration I changed the poem to this:

> *hot highway*
>
> *hitchhiker sits on the curb*
>
> *in the only shade for miles*

I replaced the word *dry* with *hot* to make the image more about temperature than water, replaced *shadow* with *shade* for the same reason, and replaced the awkward *she* with *hitchhiker* because the word better captures the state of being alone on a highway and it had a nice alliteration with the words *hot* and *highway*. I abandoned the traditional 5-7-5 form so that I could achieve a better rhythm, but I still kept the poem to seventeen syllables, I still kept myself out of it, and I left it in the present tense. There is no longer a seasonal word, but the temperature words give some idea of the season. The result, I believe, is a better haiku.

The Japanese are sticklers for rules. And this insistence on proper etiquette, rules, manners, behavior, has produced a rich and interesting culture. If you spend any time reading about haiku you will quickly realize that the form is defined by many rules. Don't let this intimidate you. The rules will help you express your own haiku moments in time-tested ways. Surprisingly, the rules for writing haiku also help you notice the haiku moments more often. Writing poetry is something everyone can do, and haiku is no exception. If you have experienced haiku moments and wish to share them with others, or if you simply wish to move peak experiences beyond the clutch of mimetic desire to haiku memory, the following tips may be helpful:

1. Carry a notebook at all times and write down images you see that make you think of haiku.
2. Discipline yourself to notice what makes moments special.
3. Capture the details.
4. Write them down in seventeen syllables, or less.
5. Compare, contrast, and associate images to re-create the moment that captured your attention.

By following these simple suggestions you will find that you notice things more, and appreciate small events that you previously missed.

Bringing haiku mind to everything

The Japanese have shown that the qualities contained in haiku and those described in Chapter 8 can be applied to gardening, pottery, papermaking, watercolor, architecture, cuisine, film-making, and dance, to name a few. All forms of writing benefit from a wabi sabi mindset. When you pare down fluff, excess, and clutter in a piece of writing, you improve it. When you describe the details of a scene, it comes alive. And when you rephrase sentences to make them clearer, you experience the delight of editing. Haiku is perhaps the most obvious media for the wabi sabi artist, but other media that move you to express yourself can achieve the same goal.

One time while browsing through a rural art shop, I came upon a framed print of Robert Duncan's *Ripe Tomatoes*. The image depicts a small boy eating a tomato in a field with a young woman carrying a basket of tomatoes and looking fondly at the child. The painting captures this remarkable moment in loving detail and communicates all the juiciness and warmth intact. I stood mesmerized at first by the redness of the fruit, and, like Lewis, I was filled with a longing. I confused the feeling with the simple desire to own the painting, or to own a farm, but some years afterward when I decided to find the print again, I realized that I didn't want the print so much as what the print subtly conveyed, what the Japanese call *yūgen*, the profound mystery of things. I wanted the feeling captured in the painting, more than the image itself. I wanted summer, and childhood, and rurality, and tomato-ness. And I wanted to go on wanting those things. In a way I knew that if I really were to receive them, it would break the magic of wanting them.

The artist may never know when his or her work will touch someone in this way. There are many reasons for the artistic impulse, but the knowledge that your work may impact someone in this way must surely be one of them. By being more in touch with the significant moments, by noticing and recording them, you will be sharing in the uncovering of that mystery behind all beauty.

Wabi sabi minds appreciate haiku moments. Wabi sabi minds practice identifying the essential elements of an experience. Haiku's extremely short form ensures that the poem contains only the essentials. This is the value of practicing the traditional form, but you need not limit the wabi sabi mind to writing haiku. You can apply the same creative impulse to almost any area of interest.

A friend lives on a sailboat he built himself. In the same way that a poet limits herself to the small space inside haiku, my friend constructed the interior of the cabin in the limited space inside the hull of the boat. It forced him to design the cabin area with attention to every detail and consider every inclusion.

Now, as he lives within his art, he feels the satisfaction wabi sabi brings. Like Rikyu in his small tearoom, the boat builder constructed an environment of elegant simplicity. The galley has storage space that is easy to use. When a shaker of spice is used it is put back easily where it belongs. The built-in seats, cupboards, and racks are all lovingly handcrafted in natural wood. Someone building a large house would find such attention to detail prohibitively expensive, both in time and money, but in the small space of the boat it is a necessary art.

Living on the boat also allows my friend to drop his kayak into the water and be out in nature within minutes. Building and living on a boat may not be for you, but any home can benefit from an aesthetically pleasing environment crafted in a small space.

Some years ago the number of photo albums accumulating in our house dismayed me. Scrapbooking was just making its big splash among those who could afford the expensive acid-free books and supplies. I observed friends enthusiastically trimming their photos to create thematic collages. They used premade templates, stencils, stickers, and fancy tools to assemble scrapbooks of color and grandeur. This wasn't what I had in mind, but I did like the idea of sorting through the vast collection of photos we had amassed to find the ones that captured the moments worth remembering. Using a wabi sabi sensibility, I spent several happy hours condensing my childhood photo collection and photos of my parents and grandparents into one book of simple design that allows access to the images without overly ornate distractions. The guiding principle in my mind was always, "what can I add to the collection of photos that will explain or complement them without being a distraction?"

I have mentioned the wabi sabi effect of smooth stones on the human nervous system and the sweet spots of nature where water, land, and air meet. You might not have direct access to these locations on a regular basis. If that is the case, consider creating a shoreline experience in an aquarium at home. Spurn the gaudy fish tank fixtures and painted gravel at the store and gather stones from any nearby shoreline instead. A water filter produces the burbling sound of a natural stream. It may take some patience to establish a healthy community of fish; colonies of invisible bacteria essential for the health of the fish fluctuate in natural rhythms and plants grow and develop over months. My aquarium gives me the same calm attention I feel on the shores of a beautiful lake near my home.

Many activities are naturally suited to wabi sabi creativity.

Winemaking, candle making, and furniture making take natural products and craft them over time into things of beauty. Carefully aged wine pleases the senses, beeswax candles benefit the air in ways that synthetic candles do not, and nothing complements a home like handmade wooden chairs and bookcases.

Some wabi sabi artists work with natural processes themselves: the growth of crystals and rust, the reactions of chemicals in glazes, the effect of weather on wood, the placement of stone in chimneys and walls, the inclusion of natural fibers in clothing, the placement of flower petals in paper, and the treatment of concrete with acid and natural stains. The wabi sabi way encourages you to connect with natural elements, create with natural patterns, and reflect nature as you go. Like a Japanese watercolor artist expressing a grove of bamboo with the seven simple strokes of the brush, you can capture your own grove of images by trusting wabi sabi beauty to guide you.

The poet Taigi touched on the motivation for sharing our connections with nature:

flitting firefly

"look, right there . . ." I start to say

but I am alone

Like Taigi pointing out the fireflies, woodworkers bring our attention to the grain of the wood when they increase the depth of the patina with shape and polish, potters highlight the elements of Earth with glazes that crack in natural patterns, and you can uncover the beauty of your own view on the world when you allow wabi sabi to guide you.

Taigi knew what woodworkers and potters know—wabi sabi moments and creations are for sharing, become more beautiful by being shared and used, and continue to enrich life with their natural presence.

Ten
Deeper wabi sabi

each wave

washes

my hands

THE BITE IN THE AIR, the smell that crisp October wind brings, the earth moist and pungent, ripe grapes scenting the air, the mossy wet aroma of decay and the leaves coming on like paper lanterns, dressing for death in colors of sun and blood; this is autumn, the most wabi sabi season of all.

The latest theory suggests that the colors of fall leaves are signals to discourage insects. It is as if the tree is saying, "See how healthy I am. I can go to bed early this fall because I have lots of resources to fight you off with." Whatever the message, bugs do seem to avoid the most brightly arrayed trees. This is, so far, the only survival advantage anyone has been able to come up with for such brilliant and vibrant shades of red, yellow, and orange that appear once each year.

We have a broad-leaf maple tree in our backyard, which produces truly impressive leaves, some measuring 17 inches or more across. While sitting in a chair by our window one late windless afternoon in October, I looked out on this tree and heard a hollow snap as one of the giant leaves broke away from the tree, and then heard only silence as it glided down toward the ground with aerodynamic grace. Over the course of the next few weeks, I watched a maple tree across the small field behind our house change from green to yellow in a steady progression from the top down. Once the transformation was complete, the leaves began to fall away from the top of the tree and continued to the bottom.

This process of stripping first the greenness, then the leaves them-selves, reveals a deep effect of wabi sabi. There is a grace in falling leaves, a gentleness in the loss of foliage.

This process begins when the tree redirects water and other nutrients away from the leaves and toward the roots. Without these supplies and the temperatures and light of summer, the leaf cannot produce energy and as the master molecule chlorophyll ceases to function, other more hardy molecules, carotene and xanthophylls, shine from behind. Sunlight also transforms sugars left in some leaves into anthocyanin, a pigment that gives leaves the color of bright red or warm rust. Tannins, the protective chemicals in oak leaves, give them more subdued colors. And as the leaves on all these trees dry, the trees seal off all contact with the stems, the brittle connective tissue weakens, and the leaves break away in the wind and rain.

Since I was a child I wondered why such beauty was linked hand in hand with loss, wondered why the grand lights of autumn shone so briefly. But it is a part of the natural process of preparing for winter; the leaves form a blanket for the tender forest-floor plants and animals, which benefit from this generous gift from the trees.

More recently I have come to see that fall reflects an impor-tant value. It is the shining value of transition. It is the value of *wu wei*, of letting go of one stage in life and moving to the next. In this grand yearly display the trees remind me that each season has its time and that the most advantageous thing to do with leaves that cannot last the winter is to let them go.

The rich golden hues of autumn represent not the gold of

coin and commerce, but the gold of a more ephemeral currency, a gold that spends itself as a gift back to the forest. It is the gold of survival, the simple mindless efficiency of a technique that works. It is a sort of natural wisdom learned without consciousness, by trees that manage to shine even as they prepare for the hardship of winter. I am reminded of Solomon, the wisest of all biblical characters, who was praised by God for choosing wisdom over wealth. And along with wisdom, wealth was given to him as well.

As we grow older we discover that our most important experiences can be rarified, our life lessons distilled, and our choices matured even as our youthful glory fades. The leaves that seemed so important, the outer foliage that we thought defined who we were, falls away and leaves us bare to the winter winds with a subtler kind of beauty. This can be devastating for those trying to hang on to summer, or youth, or prestige, or position, or privilege. Yet for those who have felt the change of temperature, who have responded to the longer lines of light, who have prepared for the change by redirecting energy toward the roots of their lives, it can be the most spiritual time of life. Just as maple sap descends from the leaves to the roots, so our own rich knowledge can travel from our heads to our hearts. And just as maple sap can be reduced to sweet syrup, our knowledge can be reduced to wisdom.

The Chinese say, "To attain knowledge, add something every day; to attain wisdom, remove something every day." As I move further into wabi sabi, I see that loss can help attain wisdom. Along with the sad losses of life there are also the liberating losses of pride, and fear of what others will think. By realizing that the leaves of life come and go, a person is free to focus energy in the deep and earthy storehouse that trees call roots and we call our soul.

Ways to naturalize your spiritual life

I'm in a bead shop in downtown Victoria, the funky old quarter with the artsy shops, the kite shop, and the used-book stores. All those used books contain the pressure of a thousand thoughts, contained within covers, waiting to be mined. But today instead of dwelling on the flat sure pages of a book, I stand on a question, on a blade, on an edge, about to fall into an answer. Long tables designed with a latticework of small cubicles contain beads, findings, and pendants. At the pendant table, each cubbyhole contains objects rendered in silver, or brass, or pewter. I look down and see multiple copies of a Celtic knot, a cloverleaf, a skull, a basketball, two crossed swords, a die, a Buddha, a Tahitian god, a stylized dog, a gnome, an eagle, a crystal, a swastika, and a yin and yang symbol. There are three kinds of crosses, each in its own cubicle and next to them an ancient European goddess like the ones found in old French caves, with an exaggerated distorted form. My fingers skip from slot to slot, finally resting on a treble clef. There is music in this shop—the clack of beads rolling in their slots, the murmur of people discussing their projects, the rising hiss as beads zip to the end of their strings and rest with the ones already there. The pendants in front of me clink pleasingly as I lift them and then replace them. I have no difficulty recognizing the symbols; they clearly represent much larger realities.

I am in a bead shop because I am on a quest. While watching the movie *Seven Years in Tibet* I became enamored with the long string of beads the Dalai Lama seemed always to have with him, wrapped impressively around his right arm. Also, I remember being in a hospital as a child and watching a nervous woman calming herself by silently saying the rosary, running the rosary beads through her fingers, the rest of the dark beads swaying below her hands. I decided to make my own prayer beads, a choice deeper than thought.

Prayers are chainless stones, pliable and visceral, that roll up from porous depths and make spaces between themselves on the thin strong string of intuition. We know these prayers by feel. We pray these prayers by feel; our fingers connect each round we touch with its hidden spherical twin. Prayer beads, used by Catholics, Buddhists, and Hindus, symbolically remind us to release each prayer from its stony human casing back to the rock that is higher than high.

I first examined premade rosary beads and found them unsatisfactory. The ones I could afford seemed too new, too artificial, with their plastic and glass beads, sharp and many sided. Something was telling me to make my own.

If an aviary is a collection of birds, a rosary is a collection of roses. Some rosary beads are actually made out of pressed rose petals.

The pendants in front of me at the bead store whisper their metallic music but I hesitate. Each is a symbol, each carries with it a message, written in visual code, available to me if I choose to see it and choose to identify with it.

The semiprecious stones lie in their own trays. I recognize hematite, the bloodstone, and labradorite, the stone with the stars inside. Something elemental in the stones informs my rational mind that there are other ways of knowing. Reaching out and touching these beads feels electric. They are cool, substantial, and heavy. In that moment, that wabi sabi second, I know that these are what I have been looking for. The rhythms of the earth seem concentrated in these metamorphic rocks. The blended shading hints that the metamorphic process is not kind, not gentle, not calm. These are not purely manufactured items; these are found things, turned into beauty by human attention. The subtle shades and tones created by the pressure of the earth; the pleasing shape created by the pressure of human ingenuity. Out of cold mines come the stones that used to be hot—the memory of that heat reflected in shiny translucence. One look and I know that the stone is chemically complex. For a moment I think I can see the atomic bonds, the lattice on a microscopic scale, holding the electromagnetic force, the binding laws of physics assembled into permanence.

And they are round. I try to imagine how this is accomplished, try to deduce the bead manufacturer's secret. Turning the small stones I see some of them have residual flat spots on four sides. Perhaps they are first cut into cubes and then rounded from there.

We humans are like this. We enter the world under pressure, we cry with newness, wiggle with potential, full of muscleless strength and mindless desire. Over time family nurtures our transient shape, and hardship polishes the boxish bundle, rounding us so that our inner beauty can shine out. I like the metaphor, even if flawed. I hold up the stone to the light.

The clerk, watching me, says, "That is labradorite. It's a feldspar." I look over at her. Her eyes are mottled gray and green and sparkle like the feldspar in my hand.

"Do you know the chemical components?" I ask.

She smiles, "Same as in you and me, sodium and calcium, transformed by pressure and heat into gemstone."

I pick out ten labradorite beads, one for each repetition of the rosary. I can't afford more. I look for a less expensive stone to make up the remainder of the beads. I choose sodalite whose name gives away its main chemical, sodium, which I think relates nicely to the labradorite that is also made partly of sodium. The blue and white matrix of the sodalite reminds me of the salty ocean and it is similar in coloration and constitution to lapis lazuli, the ancient Babylonian stone so valued for so long, but without the brassy pyrite specks. Poor man's lapis lazuli. This particular kind is called Princess Blue, named so because it was unearthed while Princess Margaret of England was visiting Ontario.

For most of my life I have believed that pure spirituality needs no objects. Faith has always been a product of the soul, not to be muddied in the perilous waters of touch and chant. Still the beads are stones, a natural reminder of how old Earth is and how age and pressure have shaped them into wabi sabi patterns as seasoned as any wine, and as ancient as days.

I buy the beads and make them into a mnemonic device. When I hold them and pray with them, I affirm the value of waiting for the real thing, of appreciating the process of choice. In their simple shape I find satisfaction, their roundness reminding me of Earth, the eyes, the tumble of acorns across a field. Their roundness symbolizes eternity, a rounded skin of color that wraps each moment, the ever-present outer membrane that separates us from everything else. The strand reminds me that I am part of a family. I am strung together with others. When I use the beads I think of my children and my fingers pause on each bead while my thoughts pause on each soul. And in touching each bead I am reminded to touch them. In this way my private devotions bring me back to my public relationships.

When I was looking for the kinds of beads I wanted, I settled on stone beads. As mentioned in Chapter 7, holding and rubbing smooth stones has a calming effect on the body. But this is only part of the appeal of beautiful stones.

Li

The stones I like best have depth in their smoothness. They are usually metamorphic rocks with veins and lines patterning their surface. The Chinese have valued these kinds of stones for many years. The Chinese character for the kind of patterns found in stones is pronounced *li* and appears on page 176. Jade can be white, lavender, yellow, and, of course, green. It occurs in the earth in association with serpentinized ultramafic rocks that have experienced a fair amount of pressure, heat, and metamorphism.

The thing that appeals to me most about jade and all the other stones that catch my eye when I walk along a shoreline is their strange organic patterns. White jade is rather plain and uninteresting, but the addition of miscellaneous chemicals gives it depth, interest, and character. Black inclusions lower the price of jade, but I find that their random sprinkling through the stone adds to the depth and authentic feel of the rock. These black spots and swirls can come from ureyite or other substances and make it appear more liquid or gel-like. Inclusions of needlelike rutile crystals in quartz, or the golden pyrite specks in lapis lazuli increase their value, and the sodalite I chose for my prayer beads is flecked with calcite patches of white and brown. They remind me very much of the look of clouds scattered across the surface of an ocean seen from a great height.

Li was first used to describe the natural patterns in jade, wood, water, and muscle. Since then li has taken on religious meaning because something about these patterns touches us. Li is in the flow of water around objects in a stream, or of traffic around a concrete median. It is the flow of ants along the forest floor, the pattern of fish swimming together against a current. It is the flow a flock of birds make as they weave through a forest together. It is the flow of a herd of wildebeests across the Serengeti. It is seen in the shapes of snow blown between buildings and the patterns of sand and gravel bars after the high spring waters recede. Scientists see li in the way bacteria grow, blood flows, and clouds form. It reflects the underlying Tao that flows through all things.

Li is the pattern of least resistance, the pattern of efficient grace. It is the organic soft weave of elements that coexist, the result of updrafts, downcurrents, and shifting pieces in a dynamic system. The more of these patterns you have in your life, the more you will touch the joy that underlies them.

Wu wei

As we move through life, carried often by circumstances beyond our control, we can choose how to deal with life's flow. When I was a teenager some friends and I drove to the Slocan River, where an old fire hose dangled from a railway bridge into the fast-moving current. From the shore a little way upstream we could swing out on a rope, let go, fall into the water, and then grab the fire hose on our way downstream. My first swing was exhilarating. Time suspended as the momentum of the pendulum action balanced the pull of gravity before I fell into the river; then came the liquid rush of bubbles and water, the surprising speed of the oncoming hose, the joint-jarring contact, and the spray-filled foaming pressure as I held on against the current. When I could hold on no longer I let go and experienced the calming pleasure of riding the river without fighting against it. Further downstream the river widened and large round boulders lay under the water at just the right depth to put my feet against. As I stopped on one in mid-stream, leaning with all my might against the onrush of water, I saw just how far downstream I had come. My friends were mere dots in the distance. I decided to swim for shore, angling with the current and arriving on dry land hundreds of feet downstream.

Walking back up the trail to make another jump, I watched friends being swept downstream, as I had been. One friend was trying to swim against the current. He was strong and a good swimmer but seemed to be making little headway against the rushing water. Finally, exhausted, he turned and angled downstream, coming to shore near where I had. I made a conscious decision at that time to remember this image and learn from it. Later while studying the Taoist idea of the waterway, I remembered that day and the tangible lesson of being immersed in a watery flow. Taoists reject self-assertiveness and competition. Extolling the self-evident nature of *wu wei,* or doing without doing, Taoists attempt to reduce the friction we usually experience from overattention to the obstacles in the stream and rely instead on the stream itself. If we notice the stream and the *li* of the stream we can relax and let it carry us, angling our effort from one shore to the other, depending on where we want to be.

The power of the phrase, "I noticed"

Teacher and school consultant Jim Fay taught me that *noticing* can have more value in building self-concept in children than praise. Noticing gives a child reality. In practicing it I found it was good for me, too. "I noticed you cleaned your desk," draws both my attention and the child's attention to the job well done. "I notice you left that problem unsolved," avoids the value judgment that exists in the more common, "You didn't do problem eight." Not that judgments in themselves are wrong. No one can go through life without accumulating a series of values and judgments about what is good and what is not. Yet if we learn to be as nonjudgmental as possible, we become like swimmers who relax and swim with the current or across it instead of fighting it. The child who is noticed, rather than judged, will learn to swim in the river of life with more awareness. She will learn the value of noticing and, in noticing, make her own judgments.

In *wu wei* we find the time to question the motivation of each action. In this moment of consideration we have the opportunity to just notice. Lately just noticing has filled me with gratitude and appreciation for the people around me. The delay in my response allows them to jump ahead, answering their own questions and suggesting their own solutions. This is wabi sabi, resting in the act of seeing and listening, reclining in the stream with your senses open. It is not easy to listen actively because most people's thoughts travel about four times faster than clear speech. So while we listen to a person talk, our brains dart about in the free time left over. In order to enter more fully into listening, I try to suspend my anticipation about what a person will say next, focusing on nonverbal cues and signals that form the undercurrent of communication.

Noticing will reward you almost as much as haiku moments. Once we start really listening to people on multiple levels instead of trying to impress them with our own greatness, we start to have a different relationship with them and with the rest of reality. The *wu wei* stream at first seems passive, almost lazy, but like wabi sabi itself, its first impressions can deceive. When life flows through us in attentive wonder, we let the unnecessary parts dissolve and flow away and instead guide perception to what matters.

Effectiveness

Wu wei is sometimes referred to as pure effectiveness. When we let assertiveness and competition wane in our souls, a clearer understanding of each task at hand emerges. If we desire efficacy over dominance, if we wish to swim with the stream of reality, rather than against it, then our actions will require less effort and we can enjoy the process.

Animal trainers who seek first to understand the animal and how it responds, before attempting to harness it, take this kind of approach. Horse-whisperer Monty Roberts is perhaps the most celebrated example of this kind of trainer. In his book *The Man Who Listens to Horses,* Roberts makes clear that listening and close attention do more to gentle an animal than training. Instead of breaking an animal, an animal whisperer enters into a relationship with it, establishing a common goal with it. Roberts has been known to tame wild stallions in a single session.

Individuals who wish to lead and motivate others can practice this subtle art by simply noticing how much they do not know. The right questions will show you *wu wei* in human relationships. A careless authority might bellow out, "Why haven't you done what I asked you to do? Get it done by the time I return." The careful leader might say instead, "I notice this task has yet to be completed. What would it take for you to accomplish this goal?" Using "what" questions instead of "why" questions can have a powerful effect, because "why" questions imply blame, whereas "what" questions do not. This kind of subtle change can redefine greatness and improve effectiveness.

The patterns behind wabi sabi

Wabi sabi values an efficient kind of beauty, such as the efficiency that underlies the beauty of minimal surfaces. A minimal surface is a "shortest distance between two points" structure that springs into existence when, for example, you dip a bent coat hanger into soapy water and then lift it out. The surface of the bubble that forms is either straight or saddle-shaped, depending on the shape of the bent hanger. Mathematicians have demonstrated that this "beauty of efficiency" underlies a good number of modern sculptures. Clean curves and pleasing shapes that form naturally with the least investment of energy and resources attract us.

The Golden Ratio

A mathematical equation known as the Golden Ratio, or Golden Section, forms the basis of many shapes in nature. The arrangement of rose petals, the arrangement of sunflower seeds in a sunflower, the branching of leaves on a stem, the flight path of diving falcons, the spiral shape of shells, the spiral shape of galaxies, the breeding patterns of rabbits, and the pleasing shapes of Frank Lloyd Wright's architecture all follow the Golden Ratio. Once you know what the Golden Ratio is you will start to see it all over the place. The irrational number phi (Φ) is called the Golden Ratio, or Golden Number (1.6180339887 . . .). Euclid first described this number as a straight line cut into extreme and mean ratios, dividing a line into two sections, a longer one and a shorter one. The longer section of the line relates to the smaller section in a unique way—the ratio of smaller section to the larger section matches the ratio of the larger section to the whole line. In other words, the smaller section fits into the larger section in the same way that the larger section fits into the whole line.

It looks like this:

We can expand this relationship to a rectangle in which the ratio of length to width is equal to phi. This means that one part of the rectangle is square while the other is rectangular, in fact the same dimension of the rectangle as the whole. It looks like this:

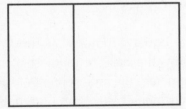

achieve the following:

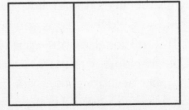

And so on:

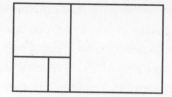

Each time you take a large square bite out of the rectangle, it leaves a phi rectangle behind. The spiral we see in shells and galaxies transits through each square of the Golden Ratio:

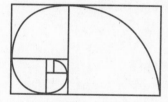

No mathematical equation describes nature more comprehensively than phi. It is the basis for the golden sequence and the golden tree, structures related to fractals.

Fractals are patterns that have the same sequence on different scales. Artificially generated fractals like the Mandelbrot set gained media attention a few years ago because of their extraordinary beauty. Mandelbrot himself came to his formulations after realizing the importance of self-similarity in plants and trees.

Fractals display self-similarity because they have a similar appearance at any magnification. If you look at the general shape of a tree, or the branching structure of the limbs, or the veins in the leaves, or the shape of the roots and rootlets, they all follow a similar pattern. A small part of the structure looks like the whole structure. Trees and ferns exhibit it, as do nonorganic structures such as clouds and coastlines. Even the apparently random splotches of paint in Jackson Pollock paintings show fractal proportion under computer analysis. This regularity appeals to us at a nonrational level. I remember my father commenting to me as a child that an abstract painting in our house appealed to him because it reminded him of a swamp. It seems that my father intuitively understood the fractal similarity. Imitation paintings of Pollock's work by lesser artists are less appealing because they lack the fractal quality and predictability.

A way with dust

Nature is beautiful and imitation of nature succeeds in beauty to the degree that it exhibits self-similarity, the Golden Ratio, and other such factors. But much in nature surpasses mathematics' ability to describe. Perhaps the sheer number of variables gives nature its appeal. Computer-generated ferns are too perfect; we tend to prefer the gnarled character of natural trees to their sanitized computer cousins. Like the impurities in jade and the cracks in Raku pottery, the multiple forces and factors that act in nature give unexpected depth to the ever-present math.

Wabi sabi does not deny the power of symmetry and simple equations that explain so much. It celebrates the wonder of a world where great complexity rises from simple rules, and it applauds the quest to understand beauty and the beautiful world around us. But wabi sabi goes further; it accepts complexity as it is given. It knows that a perfect map of the world is the world itself. Rather than seeking perfection it looks for the artistry involved in capturing nature's essential beauty. What is the least amount of information that will still communicate this essence? The wabi sabi person doesn't dip his or her life in the soap of nature and wonder what shape the bubble will be. The shape of the bubble will follow rules similar to those that produce minimal surfaces. What we can do is work on the life that produces the bubble, metaphorically twisting our wire frame and shaping it one way or the other.

No magic formulas will make your life instantly or permanently beautiful. Phi will not do it. Wabi sabi will not do it. But the wabi sabi way keeps those who follow it from sliding into that kind of thinking. It teaches humility, because we see our own beauty in context. The beauty of our youth declines, but it can give rise to a beauty of the soul—a wabi sabi soul that finds beauty in dust and sharpens small daily images into haiku moments through which subtle light can shine.

Like the leaves falling away from the trees, dust falls away from everything. It would be silly to try to keep our skin from shedding cells. Our bodies make new cells, and trees make new leaves in the spring. This is the spiritual side of wabi sabi, learning to let go of what you cannot keep and to embrace each new stage of life by allowing the previous stage to harden into bark, wood, or memories. That is the structure, which allows for further growth, the structure upon which new life depends. Jesus said it this way:

"Whoever clings to this life will lose it, and whoever loses this life will save it." Lao Tzu puts it this way: "If you realize that you have enough, you are truly rich. If you stay in the center and embrace death with your whole heart, you will endure forever."

Suggested Reading

Chan, Peter. *Bonsai Masterclass* (New York: Sterling Publishing Co., Inc., 1987).

Csikszentmihalyi, Mihaly. *Flow: The Psychology of Optimal Experience* (New York: HarperCollins, 1990).

Fay, Jim. *Shaping Self-Concept: Turning Kids into Enthusiastic Learners,* audiocassettes (Golden, Colo.: Love and Logic Institute, Inc., 1999).

Koren, Leonard. *Wabi Sabi for Artists, Designers, Poets & Philosophers* (Berkeley: Stone Bridge Press, 1994).

Krech, Gregg. *Naikan: Gratitude, Grace, and the Japanese Art of Self-Reflection* (Berkeley: Stone Bridge Press, 2002).

Le Guin, Ursula K. *Lao Tzu: Tao Te Ching: A Book about the Way and the Power of the Way* (Boston: Shambhala Publications Inc., 1997).

Maitland, Derek. *5,000 Years of Tea* (New York: Gallery Books, 1982).

Meilaender, Gilbert. *The Taste for the Other* (Grand Rapids: William B. Eerdmans Publishing Co., 1978).

Mitchell, Stephen, *Tao Te Ching: A New English Version* (New York: HarperCollins, 1988).

Natural Home. Bimonthly magazine and Web site. _www.naturalhomemagazine.com._

Petroski, Henry. _The Pencil: A History of Design and Circumstance_ (New York: Alfred A. Knopf, 1990).

Ray, Paul H. _The Cultural Creatives: How 50-Million People Are Changing the World_ (New York: Harmony Books, 2000).

van den Heuvel, Cor. _The Haiku Anthology,_ 3rd ed. (New York: W. W. Norton, 2000).

Visser, Margaret. _Since Eve Ate the Apple, Much Depends on Dinner_ (Toronto: McClelland and Stewart, 1986).

About the Author

Richard Powell was first introduced to the Japanese poetic tradition by poet and travel writer, David McFadden. After completing his course of studies in creative writing at the David Thompson University Centre, Powell moved with his wife to Vancouver Island where he obtained a degree in psychology from the University of Victoria.

A ten-year struggle with a stress-related illness led him back to Japanese aesthetics. The tranquility and peace he found strolling in Japanese gardens, reading and writing haiku, and examining Raku pottery convinced him that there was something within these art forms that he needed to understand more fully. He finally discovered an exposé on wabi sabi in a book about Japanese papermaking and realized with great joy that this was what he had intuitively known and identified with most of his life. Wabi sabi provided the context he needed to describe his values and priorities to others.

Powell explains that *Wabi Sabi Simple* is the natural extension of that discovery and invites readers to purposefully incorporate wabi sabi into their lives so that it can have the same effect on them as it has had on the arts of Japan, and on the many other works of art and culture that reflect its subtle beauty.

Powell works for Island Christian Care Society, an organization that provides shelter and care for the homeless and hard-to-house. In his spare time, when not writing or tending his bonsai, Powell explores and photographs the natural world with family and friends, drinks tea, and reads books. For more information, follow the links at *www.stillinthestream.com*.